The Macroeconomics of Global Imbalances

This book is the result of a workshop on the effects of globalization on Asian and European countries, organized by Marc Uzan and the Austrian Ministry of Finance in April 2006. Bringing together key academics, policy makers and private market participants, these chapters cover the current debate of global imbalances and the way to resolve the disequilibrium in the international monetary system and understand the need for international cooperation among the different monetary areas of the world.

Various important points come out of the book; first there is an emphasis on the difficulties for Europeans and Asians to find common positions vis-à-vis global imbalances due to different exchange rate regimes throughout Asia preventing similar responses. The role of the US dollar as a world currency is also discussed, as well as EU regional monetary cooperation and an analysis of the Euro. The implementation of economic policy to redress global imbalances is also considered, as is the emergence of China on the world stage and its industrial development projects. These questions and the way the international financial community will resolve them, will have a huge impact in the functioning of the international monetary system. The current unwinding of the global imbalances that we are facing with the global market disruptions since August 2007, demonstrate that a new geography of international finance is emerging between Europe and Asia. The book addresses also the way that a dialog in the field in monetary arena needs to be structured between Europe and Asia.

Contributions in this book are wide and far reaching and will be of interest to students and researchers engaged with the international monetary system, financial markets and macroeconomics, as well as financial policy makers across the world.

Marc Uzan is Executive Director and founder of the Reinventing Bretton Woods committee, a think tank focusing on the international financial architecture issues through a regular dialog between markets and governments. He is the author of *Financial System Under Stress* (1996) and co-editor with Dominic Wilson of the book *Private Capital Flows* (2000) also published by Routledge.

Routledge Studies in the Modern World Economy

The Macroeconomics of Global Imbalances

European and Asian perspectives

Edited by Marc Uzan

Routledge
Taylor & Francis Group

LONDON AND NEW YORK

First published 2009 by Routledge
2 Park Square, Milton Park, Abingdon, Oxfordshire OX14 4RN

Simultaneously published in the USA and Canada
by Routledge
711 Third Avenue, New York, NY 10017

First issued in paperback 2014
Routledge is an imprint of the Taylor and Francis Group, an informa business

Typeset in Times New Roman by Keyword Group Ltd.

British Library Cataloguing in Publication Data
A catalogue record for this book is available from the British Library

Library of Congress Cataloging in Publication Data
A catalog record has been requested for this book

ISBN 978-0-415-77469-7 (hbk)
ISBN 978-0-415-76219-9 (pbk)
ISBN 978-0-203-88902-2 (ebk)

Contents

Figures

Tables

Contributors

Kurt Bayer, Deputy Director General for Economic policy and International Affairs Ministry of Finance, Austria.

Josef Christl, Executive Director, Oesterreichische National Bank

Miranda Goeltom, Senior Deputy Governor, Bank of Indonesia

Masahiro Kawai, Dean, Asian development Bank Institute

Jacques de Larosière, Adviser to the Chairman, BNP Paribas.

Yung Chul Park, Professor of Economics, University of Seoul

Richard Portes, Professor of Economics, London Business School and President of the Center For Economic Policy Research

Nouriel Roubini, Professor of Economics, NYU

Jeffrey R. Shafer, Managing Director Citigroup

Shinji Takagi, Professor of Economics, Osaka University

Angel Ubide, Director of Global Economics, Tudor Investment Co.

Marc Uzan, Executive Director, Reinventing Bretton Woods Committee

Charles Wyplosz, Professor of Economics, Graduate Institute of International Studies, Geneva

Introduction

Marc Uzan and Kurt Bayer

Austria's EU presidency during the first half of 2006 also brings about the organization of an ASEM Finance Ministers' meeting in Vienna, in April 2006. As is usual, such meetings are preceded by a deputies' meeting, scheduled to prepare the agenda for the ministers' meeting. The Austrian Ministry of Finance had the idea to ask Marc Uzan of the Reinventing Bretton Woods Committee to help organize a workshop on the effects of globalization on Asian and European countries, in order to provide input of substance to the deputies' meeting. Marc enlisted the help of the Euro 50 Group, the MoF enlisted the help of the Austrian National Bank for the ensuing workshop which took place on 19, Jan. 2006 in the 'Kassensaal' of OeNB.

Two main topics were supposed to be discussed by a carefully chosen group of academics, policymakers, bankers and other experts, both from Asia and Europe: the macroeconomic relations between EU and the Asian countries and the 'emerging new division of labor' with its impacts on delo-calization, outsourcing and jobs. While the emphasis lay on the first topic (namely the large number of papers pertaining to that issue), a spirited debate was also held on the 'real economy' effects.

The workshop benefited greatly from the participation of luminaries Robert Mundell, Jacques de Larosiere, Alexandre Lamfalussy and Edmond Alphandery, among many others. In a spirited keynote speech before the pre-dinner at a typical Austrian 'Heuriger' restaurant, Richard Portes analyzed global imbalances and chided the Europeans for their very defensive position vis-à-vis increasing voice and participation of emerging and developing countries in the IMF and World Bank.

The different contributions by the lead speakers on globalization effects outlined the difficulties for Europeans and Asians to find common positions vis-à-vis global imbalances, because each country's position is quite different and stressed portfolio composition effects and rate of return differences on foreign assets are highly relevant for exposure to exchange rate fluctuations.

Analyses showed that exchange rate regimes in Asia differed strongly and thus prevented (so far) common responses to imbalances. Discussion centered also on the singular role the U.S. Dollar played as a world currency, thus offering the U.S. an additional – and very important – degree of freedom for financing their debt. The positive example of EU regional monetary cooperation with the creation of the Euro was analyzed and the role of budget balances as an important instrument for influencing current account balances quoted.

In the session on the 'real' economy effects of globalization, pressures on the European Social Model were analyzed by different typologies of the Social Models, which were classified according to a two-dimensional matrix, efficiency and equity parameters. A European industrialist and investor predicted (gloomily) that in 20 years China/Asia would produce most of the manufactured goods for the world, and Europe would have to find ways to produce high-value services and export them to the rest of the world. The stunning Chinese industrial development projects were used as an example of Asian catching-up and competition to traditional European strengths.

The format of the workshop was very conducive to strong participation in the general discussion. As usual, too little time was left for floor discussion, but nearly all participants intervened.

In what follows we have collected the papers and presentations by the lead speakers and included a short summary of the discussions. The papers/presentations are in their original (draft) form and vary from formulated papers, to speaking points, to earlier published papers, to power point presentations. It was decided, for the sake of expediency, to keep the papers in this original form and to make them available to an interested audience as soon as possible.

Marc Uzan and Edmond Alphandery and their teams are to be thanked for organization of input of substance, the Austrian National Bank and the Austrian Ministry of Finance for the excellent organization and financing of the meeting.

1 Issues for the Europe-Asia monetary and financial dialogue

Richard Portes

These remarks will focus on ASEM (the Asia-Europe Meeting) and its relevance to current issues in the international financial system. I well recall speaking at an ASEM meeting in London eight years ago. In early 1998, the Asian financial crisis was still acute, while Europe was occupied by preparations for the introduction of the euro in 1999. Since then, we have seen major developments in the two regions:

- Despite the skeptics, there has been no euro crisis. Even the euro exchange rate, whose weakness in 1999–2001 was inexplicably regarded as some negative indicator of the validity and viability of the single European currency, is now somewhat higher against the dollar than it was in January 1999. We have seen a major success: the historically unique, technically difficult creation of a single currency replacing twelve national currencies; and monetary union has played the key role in creating large, deep capital markets in the euro area.
- Asia, too, has confounded the skeptics who saw the 1997–1998 crisis as evidence of deep structural flaws and mistaken economic strategies of the Asian economies. There was a remarkable V-shaped recovery in Asia, and most Asian countries are now well protected against future crises, partly by a huge accumulation of foreign currency reserves.
- Along with the Chiang Mai agreement and the Asian Bond Fund, we have heard much discussion of possible deeper Asian monetary cooperation, even of eventual monetary unification.

With this background, what are the main issues for the Europe-Asia monetary and financial dialogue? I believe the value added in ASEM can come not just from cooperation between the two regions, but also from their jointly questioning the 'Washington consensus' in these matters. (Here I mean a combination of the US Treasury and the conventional wisdom of the Washington policy establishment, rather than the early 1990s development agenda.) It may be difficult to agree on joint views, but I do not think we shall see significant movement in well-entrenched positions unless Asia and Europe are together willing to challenge the existing order.

There are several characteristics of the current situation that we should bear in mind when considering the issues:

- Asian 'fear of floating' – that is, a predilection for exchange rate stability (evidently shared by Europe, except for the few countries that have opted to stay out of the single currency – and even Denmark shadows the euro)
- The Asian countries also fear the IMF, from their experience of IMF policies during the Asian crisis
- Under a convention that all but the United States and Europe would like to change, the Europeans provide the Managing Director of the IMF – but that, and the disproportionate European quotas in the Fund, do not prevent ...
- ... excessive American influence in IMF policies and decisions.

These factors condition Asian and European views on the three major topics that I shall cover: global imbalances; monetary arrangements in Asia and the European experience; and IMF reform.

Global imbalances – causes, sustainability, remedies

Are the current global imbalances due to an Asian 'investment strike' or 'savings glut'? I think this is not a helpful way of looking at the causes of the US current account deficit and the Asian accumulation of reserves. American savings are inadequate, and there are excess savings outside the United States. However, the major macro variables are all endogenous, and we are unlikely to extract causality from such observations. I do not agree with those who see the current configuration of international financial flows simply as the inevitable consequence of high Asian savings and a low level of development of Asian financial markets. If that were the story, why should the intermediation not be provided as much by Europe as by the United States? The euro clearly has a substantial international currency role, second only to the dollar. And European financial markets are sufficiently broad, deep, and liquid to offer the requisite range of securities as well as banking services.

I agree with the wide consensus that the US external debt is on an unsustainable path, and that the correction will entail a substantial exchange rate adjustment. Europe and Asia should indeed discuss the problems that this adjustment will raise. Among them are the following four issues:

'Burden sharing' between the euro and Asian currencies

The popular notion that Asian pegs to the dollar put upward pressure on the exchange rate of the euro is wrong. If Asian central banks were to stop supporting the dollar, that would not immediately eliminate the US current account deficit. The Asian central banks would continue to accumulate reserves, but they would be putting them in euros, so the euro would appreciate. The Asian central banks are now an investor with an extreme portfolio preference for dollars – if that preference were to change, it is the alternative asset whose price would rise. So Europe should hesitate to endorse American pressure for substantial depreciation of the RMB (and other Asian currencies), as I suggest below.

The currency composition of foreign exchange reserves

This leads to the question why, if Asian countries must accumulate reserves because of excess savings and inefficient domestic financial intermediation, they have this extreme portfolio preference for dollars. It is not a consequence of high yields on their dollar assets – it is only recently that dollar short rates have risen above those on euros, and there has been little difference between the dollar and euro long rates. Euro-area government bond markets are now deep and highly liquid, with transaction costs no higher than on US Treasuries, and the spreads on euro-denominated corporate bonds are actually lower than comparable US spreads. So euro-area bond markets offer an appropriate alternative to dollar-denominated securities. The reserve-holding policies of the Asian central banks are difficult to justify, especially in view of the inevitability of dollar depreciation (further analysis of central bank reserve-holding policies may be found in E. Papaioannou, R. Portes and G. Siourounis, 'Optimal currency shares in international reserves: The impact of the euro and the prospects for the dollar', 2006.)

Speed of adjustment

Will the adjustment be relatively gradual, as in 1985–1987, or will there be a sudden, discrete dollar 'crash'? This depends on whether we believe the markets *expect* the coming depreciation – if they have rational expectations, then theory can justify a path of gradual depreciation, but the *appreciation* of the dollar in 2005 is evidence that they do not. If there is a significant probability of a sudden fall in the dollar, Europe and Asia should urgently be discussing how they might deal with it.

The exchange rate of the renminbi

The policy debate on Chinese exchange rate policy has been driven excessively by the American perspective and the American bilateral deficit with China. Europe and Asia should say so, jointly. It is not clear that the RMB is substantially overvalued – if capital controls were to be loosened significantly and the RMB were allowed to float, can we be confident that it would appreciate? Its effective rate in fact rose with the dollar in 2005. Sharp revaluation of the RMB with respect to the dollar is not the solution to any major problem, and it could endanger both Chinese internal stability and that of the international economy. It would be helpful, too, if not only Washington were to discuss and define what is 'currency manipulation', who practices it, and whether policy measures to deter it are justified. In addition perhaps Europe should point out what Asia (excluding China) may be reluctant to acknowledge: that much of the increase in the Chinese bilateral surplus with the United States has come in parallel with a drop in the surpluses of other Asian countries with the United States, simply reflecting changes in production and sourcing patterns within Asia.

A new plaza?

Should Europe and Asia seek agreement on the required average depreciation of the dollar and its 'distribution'? Could Europe and Asia agree? I do not think this is a sensible objective. The international financial system has changed fundamentally in the past 20 years: capital is much more mobile, cross-border flows are much greater now. The concept of 'fundamental equilibrium exchange rates' is inappropriate to such a world, because one cannot estimate 'long-term capital flows' and thereby specify the corresponding current accounts and exchange rates. The IMF has wisely refrained from proposing a grid of reference rates, and Europe and Asia should not enter into such a discussion, except perhaps to say that the long-standing views of some Washington think-tanks might require revision.

Monetary arrangements in Asia and European experience

The Asian countries have manifested considerable interest in monetary cooperation, notably with the Chiang Mai initiative and the Asian Bond Fund. I shall comment on three issues in this context.

Is there a case for a common peg?

A common peg to what? say, a dollar-euro basket; but there is a wide range of exchange rate policies in Asia – the currencies are not all pegged to the dollar, and indeed they are not currently moving together. On the other hand, the high share of intra-regional trade in total trade – higher than in the euro area – suggests a prima facie case for more currency stability than we currently see.

In the longer run, might we see a single Asian currency?

There are many characteristics of the European experience which would be difficult to duplicate in Asia. For example, the European Monetary System, at least as it operated from 1979 to the beginning of the 1990s, provided a 'running-in period' for currency cooperation. This example cannot easily be followed in Asia, because it rested partly on capital controls; when these were relaxed, the system broke down (1992–1993). Nor is there an obvious anchor currency to play the role that the deutschemark had in the progression towards the euro. Most important, perhaps, is that the Single Market programme launched in 1986 was the basis for the single currency – this was expressed well in the title of the main preparatory study for EMU: *One Market, One Money*. The Single Market was and is Europe's outstanding expression of the willingness to pool sovereignty – to accept both 'harmonization' and 'mutual recognition' of national regulations – for the sake of economic integration. It will not be easy to bring Asian countries to pool sovereignty, given the political relationships, in particular the rivalries and other tensions among the three large countries (and that is just East Asia – India and Pakistan would add further sources of potential political discord).

How important are current initiatives for monetary cooperation?

Chiang Mai is in principle a 'good thing', and it could be seen as a step on the long road towards a common currency; but it is very limited as it stands: in amounts; in being tied to the borrower's acceptance of an IMF programme; and in giving any creditor the right to opt out. To go from Chiang Mai to pooling foreign exchange reserves or an Asian Monetary Fund would require some of the same conditions as a common currency, including another aspect of pooling sovereignty that will be politically difficult: strong mutual economic policy surveillance.

IMF reform

Do we need the Fund? With the current level of excess global liquidity, this is not obvious – only a couple of major countries (Brazil, Turkey) seem at risk of an external crisis. Moreover, some other IMF activities should simply be terminated – c.g., the Fund should not take poverty reduction as one of its major objectives. This is the proper role of the World Bank. Going back to the IMF's original objectives, however, there is a current threat to international financial stability – a possible dollar crash – and there are problems of balance of payments adjustment. Such disequilibria will continue in a world of floating exchange rates and massive international capital flows. Hence there is a need for strong surveillance and willingness to criticize policies of major countries.

There are other issues regarding crisis prevention, crisis resolution and dealing with debt defaults – if you like, 'the Fund after Argentina'. With Daniel Cohen, I have proposed[1] a facility that would make the Fund the 'lender of first resort' in appropriate cases. This could be a useful addition to the crisis-prevention arsenal. Otherwise, the IMF should, in my view, take a back seat. The SDRM initiative was useful in 'unblocking' the resistance to collective action clauses, but there will not be (and, in my view, should not) be an 'international bankruptcy court', and in any case the Fund should not play a central role in debt restructuring. This is a matter for negotiation between the parties. If, as some would like, the IMF were to provide both debtor and creditors with an assessment of 'debt sustainability', that would pre-empt negotiations. The most it can do is to improve the institutional environment for orderly debt workouts.

However, we cannot go further on any of these issues without reform of IMF governance: representation on the Board and realignment of quotas. Here the major burden is on Europe, to acknowledge that the euro has changed the international as well as the internal European equilibrium. All Asia can do is to put as much pressure as possible on the Europeans!

That said, however, there is a strong case for Europe and Asia to discuss how their perspectives, coming from outside Washington, legitimately differ from the consensus in Washington that so dominates international discourse and policy-making – in my view, often wrongly.

Notes

1   *Crises de la dette: prévention et résolution*, Documentation Française (for the Conseil d'Analyse Economique, Office of the Prime Minister of France), September 2003; and 'A Lender of *First* Resort', CEPR Discussion Paper no. 4615, 2004, revised version forthcoming as IMF Working Paper. Leerseite

2 A few thoughts on global imbalances

Jacques de Larosière

The world global financial imbalances can be summarized in the following way:

1. A strong GDP growth in the US coupled with large current account deficits;
2. Subdued economic growth in Europe – hindered by insufficient structural reforms – and a balanced position in terms of current accounts;
3. A spectacular economic expansion in East Asia coupled with high current account surpluses and growing international reserve accumulation.

Let me venture a few ideas on how that highly contrasted picture can be explained and possibly improved.

A strong GDP growth in the US coupled with growing current account deficits

There is a tendency among some economists and more widely within the circle of American policy makers, to consider that imbalances in the US current account are a **consequence** of external factors and therefore do not need to be tackled by the US authorities. Since there is, according to this view, a 'global savings glut' in the rest of the world, let the 'excess savers' deal with it.

In the same vein, some are tempted to say:

'As long as productivity growth is strong and healthy, as long as inflation is contained and as long as the US GDP grows in line with its potential (around 3.5 per cent), nothing is to be worried about. Any restrictive policy action by the US would only (other things being equal) reduce global growth and damage not only the US but also the other countries that are taking advantage of the strong domestic demand in the US'.

Table 2.1 A summary of present current account imbalances as they stem from major areas

Billions of US dollars	2004	2005 (forecasts)	2006 (estimates)
USA	− 668	− 759	− 805
Euro-area	+ 46	+ 23	+ 18
Japan	+ 172	+ 153	+ 140
Asia (developing)	+ 93	+ 109	+ 113
(of which China)	(+ 68)	(+ 115)	(+ 121)
Middle East	+ 102	+ 217	+ 272
Russia	+ 60	+ 101	+ 119

Source: IMF, World Economic Outlook, September 2005.

In addition (see Table 2.1) they add that if the US continue to attract – primarily in the form of the acquisition by foreigners of US Treasury instruments – the necessary inflows of capital to finance their external deficit (around 6 per cent of GDP), it is because foreign investors are willing to do so in view of the good performance of the US economy and of US assets.

For sure, the US current account deficit is partly a result of faster growth of domestic demand in the US than in the Euro area, in Japan and in a number of emerging countries, but it is also true that the causes of US external imbalances are due to a large extent to negative **domestic** factors.

- The US fiscal deficit is a case in point. General government fiscal imbalances have hovered around − 4 per cent of GDP per year since 2002.[1] Given the dramatic decrease in savings by households, these fiscal deficits only compound the current account problems. So it would be desirable that the US government starts reining in its fiscal imbalances.
- But the major factor at play results from the insufficiency of household savings in the US.

The fact that US household savings are now negative, has to do with domestic causes:

- The accommodative monetary policy over the years that has led to low borrowing interest rates;
- the high liquidity and the bubble in asset prices with its wealth effects;
- the ability of the US households to leverage and 'extract cash' out of housing wealth through using property as collateral or through extended and renegotiated loans.

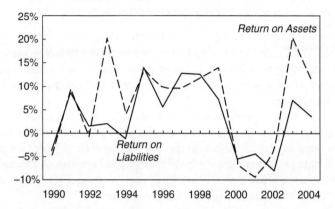

United States: Real Rates of Return on External Assets and
Liabilities (per cent)

Figure 2.1 Better return: US investors have earned more from their external assets
than foreigners have from investments in the United States.
Source: Lane and Milesi-Ferretti (2005b).

- Additionally, the notion that foreign investors are 'attracted' by higher yields on US assets than those they can expect in the rest of the world is a misconception. Recent studies show that US investments abroad have, over the last 15 years, yielded significantly more returns than those earned by foreigners who have assets in the US (see Figure 2.1).[2]

- One sometimes argues that the growing deficit in the trade of goods in the US will – because of high spending on R&D and efficient corporate innovation – be offset in part by the surplus in services. But this is not the case. The US surplus of services with the rest of the world is declining and is very small in comparison with the deficit in goods (the services surplus has declined to 0.5 per cent of GDP).[3]

- Finally, it is not sure that a significant increase in domestic demand in Japan, Europe and the Asian economies, would necessarily lead to a rebalancing of the US trade account. Indeed, the US industrial manufacturing production has been very rigid since the mid-1990s and has not reacted much to increases in domestic demand. How would it react to increases in external domestic demand – barring extreme movements in exchange rates which would have themselves negative effects on the world economy? The answer is not obvious. It may well be that an increase in domestic demand in China, for example, would be met by Chinese production and not by US exports, given the over-investment and the low costs of the Chinese economy.

Subdued economic growth in Europe – hindered by insufficient structural reforms – and a balanced position in terms of current balance of payments

First, one has to observe that there is no 'excess' savings in Europe contrary to some uninformed views. The Euro area current account is in global balance: according to ECB statistics, from 2000 to 2004 the cumulated surplus over those five years amounted only to 13 billion euros (i.e., 2.6 billion a year on average).

This trend has continued in 2005.[4] In total, if one looks at gross savings related to GDP, the Euro area in 2004 was at 20 per cent which is equal to gross fixed capital formation (in the US, figures show a 6 per cent deficit and in Japan a 2.5 per cent surplus).[5] International reserves of the euro area have remained stable over the past three years at around 300 billion euros.

So there is no overall 'savings glut' in Europe.

Second, the composition of savings and dissavings is different in Europe from the situation in the US.

- Indeed, household savings in Europe have remained positive at their historical levels (gross savings ratios to disposable income have hovered around 14 per cent over the last six years) while net household debt has remained stable.
- The corporate sector is almost in balance (9 per cent gross savings to GDP versus gross fixed capital formation of around 10 per cent), but, given improved profits, corporate indebtedness has significantly reduced over the last four years.
- Lastly, the public finances of the euro zone are in bad shape: continued deficits (close to or higher than 3 per cent) high debt ratios to GDP (71 per cent average).

So, the problem is not in the household nor in the corporate sector, but in inadequate fiscal policies.

Third, most European countries have not indulged in the housing leverage mechanisms that have so powerfully boosted consumption in the US. Residential investment in Europe has not grown as fast as in the US over the last years.

This can be explained, in part, by very different housing financing mechanisms that characterize most European countries. For example:

- the possibilities to renegotiate conditions after rate decreases are lesser than in the US;
- the possibility to 'extract cash' out of housing wealth is not a continental European practice.

Therefore Europe has not 'benefited' (if one can say!) from the residential wealth engine that has boosted consumption in the US.

What should Europe do to answer the question regarding the external responses to a rebalancing of savings in the US?

I shall focus on the following points.

First, the things Europe should NOT do:

- European countries should not increase their fiscal deficits to boost demand. The debt ratios are so high and the future consequences of aging population on social and health care systems are such that any relaxation of fiscal policies would be harmful. On the contrary, it is essential for long-term growth to regain budgetary discipline through expenditure reductions;
- European countries should not try to match the financial devices that allow households to extract cash from house price increases. The overextended position of US households is, to a large extent, a systemic weakness and continental Europe is, in this regard, in a more 'normal' or 'neutral' position, even if low interest rates (as they are now) provide a permanent temptation to get into more debt.

The things Europe should be doing:

- reforming their ailing health care and pension systems;
- opening up and liberalizing their labour and goods and services markets which are much too rigid;
- extending working hours to boost output and increase durably potential growth (which has been revised downwards to 2 per cent). Some steps have been recently taken in these directions by European Governments (public sector pensions, labour market flexibility, overhaul of public debt and fiscal expenditure…) but they need to be continued and reinforced;
- finally, energy conservation is also a structural obligation for all countries. In this respect, the nuclear energy policy that France engaged in, more than 30 years ago, has produced remarkable results (75 per cent of electricity consumption in France comes from nuclear plants) and has lessened its oil dependency.

In sum, structural reforms are a precondition to enhance the growth potential and the resiliency of European economies even if their short-term impact on global imbalances is difficult to assess.

Basically,[6] an increase in the productivity of the European Union would help to adjust the US current account deficit in as much as it were to occur in the non-tradable sector (productivity increases in the tradable sector could improve EU's trade accounts).

A spectacular economic expansion in East Asia coupled with high current account surpluses and growing international reserve accumulation

As Professor Yung Chul Park has stated in a recent paper:[7] 'At the end of September 2005, a total of reserves held by 10 East Asian economies[8] stood at $2485 billion up from a little over 1 trillion five years earlier'. China counts for close to $800 billion out of that total. This reserve increase has been the result of current account surpluses as well as of growing capital inflows coupled with heavy exchange rate intervention to stabilize Asian currencies.

The case of Japan and its relations with the other Asian countries is important to analyze: Japan's current account surplus is among the largest in the world (153 billion in 2005) and amounts to 42 per cent of the total current account surpluses of the 10 East Asian Economies listed above.

However, Japan's trade surplus with the US has 'only' amounted to 68 billion US dollars in 2005 (i.e., 28.8 per cent of the total bilateral trade balance of the 10 East Asian Economies with the US). China, on the other hand – although it has a significantly smaller global current account surplus (115 billion in 2005) than Japan – has a much larger bilateral trade surplus with the US: 166 billion, i.e., close to 50 per cent of the total of the 10 East Asian Economies.

This explains the intensity of US political reactions to the Chinese exchange rate policy and the American protectionist temptations that should not be underestimated. One also has to observe that Japan has been running surpluses in its trade with all the 10 Asian Economies including China. This situation has been accompanied by a depreciation (in real effective terms) of 15 per cent of the yen over the three-year period beginning in 2003,[9] which compounds exchange rate policy difficulties in other East Asian economies.

So, a move towards reviving domestic demand in Japan appears essential.

'Unless Japan is prepared to absorb more goods and services not only from the US but also from other East Asian countries, the external pressure on the rest of East Asia to expand domestic demand will not be headed'

(Pr. Park).

The case of China is dominated by structural issues: China's National Savings amount to 51 per cent of GDP and are expected to increase further. Is this situation – very high savings, current account surpluses and huge reserve accumulation – durable ?

Not in the long term; but in spite of the importance of defining in general terms the appropriate objectives (i.e., shifting demand in China to domestic consumption, letting more flexibility in the exchange rate, liberalizing services...), it seems more pertinent to look into the complexities of the situation and to take into account the structural aspect of issues. I shall give a few examples:

- If savings are high in a country like China, it is in part because of the deficiencies of social safety nets and retirement schemes which raises an important challenge for the authorities;
- if flexibility of the exchange rate is desirable, stability and strengthening of the financial system is also of the essence. These two objectives are closely interrelated, but at the present moment, too rapid a move towards exchange rate flexibility could compound the problems of the financial sector;
- the expansionary monetary policy in China (fuelled by heavy exchange rate interventions) tends to favour lending at regulated low interest rates which is mainly directed to existing companies in particular state-owned. This compounds the difficulty of financing new know-how and services-oriented enterprises and thus tends to weaken productivity growth, to encourage overinvestment and to increase production and the need to export;
- therefore, a more market-driven monetary policy, more flexible interest rates and efficient banks have a crucial role to play in interm-ediating the substantial savings towards productive investments and services;
- underemployment of significant parts of the rural population remains a pressing concern 'as the economy adjusts to the effects of state-owned enterprises reforms and WTO accession'.[10]

Thus, one can stress that managing successfully China's long-term growth and encouraging its gradual integration in the global economy, requires a number of structural changes that will take time.

Raghuman Rajan, economic counsellor and Director of the Research Department at the IMF[11] has remarkably summarized the issue of global imbalances:

'Some have suggested the world has a saving glut. In fact, the world is investing too little... investments have fallen off sharply since then with only very cautious recovery'.

'The policy response to the slowdown in investments has differed considerably across countries. In the industrial countries, accommodative policies such as expansionary budgets and low interest rates have led to consumption or credit-fuelled growth, particularly in the Anglo-Saxon economies. Government savings have fallen especially in the US and Japan and household savings have virtually disappeared in some countries with housing booms ...'

'We should celebrate the implicit global policy coordination that enables the world to weather this crisis... Now, (things) need to be reversed. It is misleading to term this situation as a savings glut for that would imply that countries running current account surpluses should reduce domestic incentives to save. But if the true problem is investment restraint... the world needs two kinds of transitions. First, consumption has to give way smoothly to investment, as past excess capacity is worked off and as expansionary policies in industrial countries return to normal. Second, to reduce the current account imbalances that have built up, demand has to shift from countries with deficits to countries with surpluses'.

Therefore, multiple and complex policy actions are now called for in all parts of the world.[12] If they are carried out (some have already been engaged) and if governments are seen as seriously integrating these multifaceted objectives in their own policies, the outcome could be a gradual reduction of present imbalances and vulnerabilities. Such a change in the present trends would help markets to adjust smoothly. Otherwise, developments could be uncertain, precipitous and damaging to all.

Notes

1 Against an average of 2.7 per cent in the Euro zone.
2 See: Philip Lane and Gian Maria Milesi-Ferretti: 'Examining Global Imbalances' by (Vienna – Eurogroup 50 – January 2006). See also Patrick Artus, Banque de France, Symposium – November 4, 2005. See also Chart I annexed.
3 See: Patrick Artus mentioned above.
4 Actually, there has been a deficit of 7.8 billion euros in the first three quarters of 2005 due, in particular, to Spain and France current account deterioration (ECB – Statistics).
5 2004: US gross savings: 13.8 per cent of GDP; gross fixed capital formation: 20.1 per cent. Japan gross savings: 26.3 per cent of GDP; gross fixed capital formation: 23.9 per cent.
   Source: ECB
6 See: OECD 2004 – Obstfeld and Rogoff: 'The Unsustainable US Current Account Position Revisited', Working Paper 10869. See also: Josef Christl: 'Global Imbalances and Regional Monetary Cooperation', Vienna, Eurogroup 50, January 2006.

7 'Global Imbalances and East Asia's Policy Adjustments', Eurogroup 50, Vienna, January 2006.
8 China, Japan, Korea, Taiwan, Hong Kong, Indonesia, Malaysia, the Philippines, Singapore and Thailand.
9 See: Professor Yung Chul Park above.
10 'China's growth and integration in to the world economy', IMF, Occasional Paper 232, 2004.
11 'The Age', Melbourne, September 2005, quoted by Bob Solomon in his International Economic Letter, dated November 17, 2005.
12 Including in the Middle East where much of the large current surpluses should be channelled into major investment projects notably in the energy sector.

3   A world out of balance?

Angel Ubide[1]

As the US current account deficit has climbed beyond all previous historical records, both concerns about the implications of this development and debates about possible remedies have intensified in academic and policy circles. References to the risks emanating from 'global imbalances' – which has become the politically correct synonym for the US current account deficit – have become a standard health warning accompanying most economic forecasts, and foreign exchange markets have repeatedly had the jitters. After a brief debate in late 2004, however, the excitement has been in vain: economic polices have barely changed and perceptions of the importance of the problem seem to be declining. In fact, the discussion has become largely politicized, with different consensus in the different geographical areas: the 'Washington consensus' that blames China, the 'European consensus' that blames the US fiscal deficit and the Fed's loose monetary policy, and the 'Asian consensus' that sees the accumulation of foreign exchange reserves as an integral component of their managed float exchange rate system. The side effect of this polarization is the lack of a deep analysis of the problem, as the large majority of studies are intended to pursue a specific agenda.

This note tries to fill this gap by providing a comprehensive discussion of the global imbalance; and this is badly needed, because, despite the apparent complacency, there is still a diffuse feeling among policy makers that the situation is unsustainable and that the US dollar will eventually need to fall further. Given the appreciation of European currencies against the dollar in recent years, policy makers have increasingly called on Asian countries, especially China, to allow their currencies to rise against the dollar. China's first step – a move toward a managed floating basket that involved an initial appreciation of 2.1 per cent with respect to the USD – was encouraging, but its small size despite the tremendous pressure exerted by US policy makers shows how difficult it will be to achieve equilibrium only through price adjustment. In fact, it is doubtful that exchange rate changes will suffice to restore current account imbalances to more sustainable levels. These imbalances are more deeply rooted in changes in the demand and supply of international savings which, in turn, have triggered important policy decisions in industrial and developing countries. Adjustment will therefore not only require exchange rate changes but also changes in real interest rates and, along with this, probably in asset prices.

However, let's look at the data first, because there is a tendency to look at the data with a biased view. Let's look at some of the typical figures put forward to paint the gloomy scenario. The US current account deficit is at 6 per cent of GDP, and that is a very large figure that must be unsustainable. Well, the Australian current account deficit has been of a similar magnitude for the last several years and the Australian currency has not declined, if anything it has appreciated further. The US household savings rate is zero, or even negative, and that must be unsustainable. Well, first of all there is nothing cast in stone as to what the 'right' level of savings should be; but in addition, it is clear that the savings rate, as it is defined as a per cent of disposable income not including wealth, is not very informative – the typical example being that a person cashing in some stocks sees its savings decline, as it pays capital gains taxes on it, but the increase in wealth is not accounted for. Academic studies say that a depreciation of the USD of 20–50 per cent is unavoidable, but is this really feasible? Let's think in political economy terms for a second, against who would the dollar depreciate by that amount before intervention takes place? It is much more interesting to look at the data and try to make an unbiased analysis and one fact stands out: the US current account deficit accelerates in 1997, and then again in 2001. What happened then?

The current account imbalance is in fact the result of a combination of multiple shocks staggered in time. Specifically, we argue that a rise in the international supply of savings from emerging market countries – after 1997 – combined with a fall in investment in OECD countries – after 2001 – pushed real interest rates to record lows. The deflation scare that emerged from the combination of the bursting of the stock market bubble, the shocks that ensued the corporate scandals and the geopolitical events, and the entering of China and India into the world trading system, generated a policy response leading to nominal interest rates declining sharply in line with real rates. An initial savings glut thus became a liquidity glut. While the fall in real interest rates was common to most OECD countries (and in particular to both the US and the eurozone) the impact on domestic demand was asymmetric – Japan and Europe lagging clearly behind – and, consequently, current account imbalances rose. When the sustained increase in oil prices added to the saving-investment imbalance, current account imbalances reached historical highs. It is thus wrong to blame any individual

actor for the imbalance, be it China or US fiscal policy. It is a complex
situation that will evolve in a complex way.

How does the story end? A few facts seem clear. First, there is little
appetite for policy action, both at the domestic and the global level: there is a
clear menu of policy options that each player should be undertaking *for their
own good* – that is, fiscal adjustment in the US, accelerated structural reform
in Europe, exchange rate appreciation in Asia – yet none of the players are
heeding this advice to its full extent. Thus, one should not expect any relief
from the current constellation of policy makers – or perhaps what happens is
that there is not clear need for policy action, if the current situation is the
result of a combination of multiple shocks, as advanced above. Second,
although the cyclical mechanisms of adjustment are well understood, it is
unclear how they would play out in practice. A typically advanced scenario,
whereby a confidence crisis on the US economy dries up foreign financing
and makes the dollar tumble and interest rates rise, remains a theoretical
possibility, but the market behavior over the last years seems to suggest that
it is highly unlikely.

In fact, one could characterize the US economy as a huge venture
capital fund that borrows short in its own currency and invests abroad in
FDI. The data on the International Investment Position in fact shows that
the US enjoys a positive net investment income (about 36 billion USD)
despite having a very large negative NFA position (about –2.5 trillion
USD). From this perspective, the US is a net creditor, not a net debtor,
and thus there is no problem! A deeper analysis reveals a less benign assessment. The key to this puzzle is the persistent positive return differential
on FDI. The US makes about 5 per cent more on its FDI abroad than
foreigners make on their FDI in the US. Once one looks deeper into the
numbers, the real difference is the level of retained earnings: the difference
between US-retained earnings abroad and foreign-retained earnings in the
US is about 1 trillion USD over 1989–2004. This is a puzzle that is difficult
to rationalize and that has not been explained. Such a large difference could
be the result of tax advantages or diverging corporate strategies, but it is
difficult to believe that it can be so large and persistent. These missing earnings may hold the key to the sustainability – or lack of – of the US external
position.

The most likely scenario remains one where the standard business cycle
dynamics play out in a very slow fashion. With investment recovering in
OECD countries, we believe it is only a matter of time before real and, ulti-
mately, nominal rates rise. The rise in real rates – and accompanying decline
in asset prices – would in time rebalance domestic demand across regions
and restore current account balances to more sustainable levels. This is likely
to be the key adjustment mechanism, not changes in exchange rates, and

we are seeing the beginning of it with the recent increase in yields and the improved economic outlook in Europe and Japan. If supervisors and regulators have ensured that the recent expansion in credit has been done under safe and sound criteria, and if there are no further shocks or policy mistakes, then the odds of a gradual and smooth adjustment are high. Clearly, the longer gradual real interest rate and asset price adjustments are delayed, the higher is the risk that a new shock triggers a disorderly unwinding of the imbalances that imparts serious exchange rate and asset price shocks on the world economy. While such a disruptive adjustment scenario may appear not very likely in the near-term future, it becomes ever more likely as the forecasting horizon increases, but again, the most likely scenario is a gradual, cyclically induced adjustment that last several cycles, what I label an 'opportunistic approach to the resolution of the global imbalance', similar to the anti-inflation strategies of the 80s and 90s: policy makers will adopt policies that slowly reduce the imbalance, taking advantage of the expected adustments that future economic slowdowns will bring about.

In this context it is fair to ask whether the current framework for monetary policies around the globe is adequate. In a world with ever more integrated capital markets and global supply chains, the information content of traditional domestic indicators of price pressures has declined significantly. Inflation is becoming a global phenomenon, the supply of labor is becoming largely global, and this raises the question of whether conducting monetary policy based on domestic Phillips curve considerations is still appropriate. We find indeed a strong correlation between house price inflation and current account deficits across developed countries suggesting that, in the absence of wage inflation because of global labor arbitrage, overheating appears in the external accounts. Under this hypothesis, the US current account deficit and inflated housing markets could just be indications of an overheated economy, probably as a result of an overestimation of potential growth. Thus, it looks as if the global imbalance may not be a problem per se, but it could become one if it degenerates in excessive asset price inflation. At the same time, the current account imbalance could simply be signaling different speeds of the transmission mechanism of monetary policy across countries. A number of questions thus arise: can a central bank consider its job done if it achieves internal balance at the expense of a large external imbalance? Should monetary policy be redefined as the achievement of financial stability, in a way that encompasses internal and external balances, as well as asset price stability?

The answer to these questions is key in defining what the appropriate policy response should be. If the current global imbalance is just the result of a combination of external shocks, then all actors must contribute to its resolution – and the euro area should try and stimulate its domestic demand to share the burden of the adjustment with the US, rather than considering itself an innocent bystander with a balanced economy. If instead the current global imbalance is a signal of too loose a constellation of policies in the US then the US should bear the brunt of the adjustment process – and the rest of the world should just admit that this US overheating has benefited them along the way rather than complain about the cost of the adjustment.

Notes

1 The builds on joint work with Daniel Gross and Thomas Mayer for our forthcoming CEPS Special Report, A World out of Balance.

4   Global imbalances and regional monetary cooperation

Josef Christl

Introduction

This article first addresses very briefly some basic issues of regional economic cooperation and global imbalances. Second, it will show that EMU not only shelters its member states against international shocks but also contributes to international monetary stability. Third, it will draw some policy conclusions.

Regional economic cooperation

Balassa (1962) set out a logical roadmap for the steps of regional economic cooperation and integration: In his view, countries decide first to create a free trade area. This could then lead to a common external tariff, thereby producing a customs union. Efficiencies would be further generated by the formation of a genuine internal market amongst member countries. The gains of the internal market could be best achieved through further 'deepening' of integration. Therefore, monetary integration – the use of a common currency – would be the next stage. This in turn would generate incentives for further political integration. How much political integration is required, is still an open question. In my view at least some pooling of economic policy sovereignty seems to be necessary.

The economic case when and if monetary integration should take place is based on the optimum currency area (OCA) theory, which postulates that lower transaction costs, reduced need for reserve holdings, reduction in regional price discrimination, and elimination of costs due to interregional exchange rate uncertainty must outweigh the costs of the loss of monetary policy autonomy (Mundell, 1961). In principle, the chances for making monetary union a success, are better, if you have a high degree of convergence in business cycle, flexible labour and product markets, and a high mobility of labour and capital.

Of course, by reducing transactions and information costs, a single currency itself facilitates trade and financial flows amongst members. There is a large body of evidence suggesting that a common currency stimulates trade. Rose and Engel (2002) argue that a common currency area significantly increases international business cycle correlations. Frankel and Rose (2002) and others conclude that a common currency is especially trade-stimulating. Corsetti and Pesenti (2002) formalize the theory behind this catalyzing role of monetary unions and the possibility of OCA criteria being satisfied ex-post even if they fail ex-ante. In other words, OCA criteria may be endogenous since the structure of the economy is endogenous to economic policy (Frankel and Rose, 1998).

It is clear that a common currency, as well as convergence in macro policies and micro-prudential statutes and regulations, will deepen and broaden regional financial markets and shelters to some extent from exogenous shocks. The terrible events of September 11, would have shocked Europe as a whole much more, if the monetary union had not existed at that time. This property of shelter is especially important for smaller economies and, as I said, this certainly holds true for smaller European economies that have joined EMU.

By definition, global current account imbalances are related to savings and investment decisions taken by the private and public sectors. The savings glut hypothesis brought forward by Bernanke (2005) suggests that especially Asian countries save more than they invest. If Asian market participants would spend more on domestic demand, global imbalances, i.e., the US current account deficit would be significantly reduced. In this respect two further aspects have to be pointed out: First, one has to look at the other part of the equation as well: The USA with its budget deficit and declining household savings obviously explains partly the global imbalances issue. Second, available data suggest that unusually low investment rates for this stage of the business cycle have resulted in excess savings, which – by the way – contribute to strong asset prices and low long-term interest rates. In other words, the 'savings glut' is rather a kind of 'global corporate investment gap'.

EMU's contribution to international stability

Price stability: spreading the zone of monetary stability

Since the beginning of EMU, the euro-area has achieved low inflation as well as stable and low inflation expectations. As a result, inflation risk premia and interest rates have been very low. The Governing Council of the Eurosystem has made its decisions with a view to maintaining price stability, which is the primary objective of the Eurosystem according to the EU Treaty.

Price stability is defined as 'year-on-year increases in the HICP for the euro-area of close to but below two per cent' and it is a medium-term goal. The maintenance of price stability helps to allocate resources efficiently both across uses and across time. In order to maintain price stability, the Eurosystem has designed a monetary policy strategy whereby risks to price stability are assessed on the basis of two pillars. The first pillar is a broadly based assessment of a wide range of economic and financial indicators, including various forecasts. Its aim is to identify short- to medium-term prospects for price stability from the demand side of the economy and from various shocks. The second pillar assigns a prominent role to monetary developments, reflecting the theoretical and empirical findings that excessive money and credit growth over the long run result in higher inflation. The monetary pillar thus has a medium- to long-term time horizon. It also serves to cross-check the findings of the first pillar.

Fiscal stability as a precondition for a sustainable macroeconomic savings-investment balance

Sound fiscal policies are a corner stone of the euro-area's stability architecture. The macroeconomic policies pursued in the euro-area at present are – although by far not perfect – on the whole more conducive to price stability, fiscal prudence and structural changes than at any time in the 1970s, 1980s or early 1990s. The Maastricht fiscal convergence criteria have also set a kind of standard beyond the euro-area, above all in the EU Member States which have not yet adopted the euro, including the New Member States, many of which already participate in the ERM II. The fact that the developments of all Member States' public finances are continuously checked and discussed in detail by the ECOFIN Council implies transparency, accountability and peer pressure.

The fiscal rules can act as a commitment device to prevent short-sighted political considerations leading to excessive spending and deficits and to limit discretionary fiscal policy. In a monetary union, undisciplined fiscal policies may impede a stability-oriented single monetary policy and would lead to negative spillovers. Fiscal rules are an important issue for the long-term sustainability of a monetary union (Christl 2003). Fiscal rules also matter because monetary union membership could give rise to moral hazard and free-rider problems: Moral hazard because a member country might expect to be bailed out by others when faced with unsustainable debt levels; free-riding because fiscal laxity in one country can drive up the union-wide interest rate and can induce others to relax fiscal rules.

Since market interest rate spreads have not acted as an effective deterrent against excessive deficits, fiscal rules are a necessary complement to achieve sound fiscal policies for a credible and successful monetary union. That is why strict adherence to the revised rules of the SGP is paramount to safeguarding its credibility. Fiscal rules also help to reduce fiscal profligacy in other countries in the world and would in this way help to avoid or to reduce global imbalances.

Structural reforms: creating positive growth and employment spillovers for the rest of the world

In the long run, structural reforms are the only way to enhance the growth potential and improve the resilience of economies against shocks. Therefore, structural reforms summarized in the Lisbon Agenda are a key priority for policymakers in Europe and also for the Austrian Presidency. The main rationale for structural reforms is to create dynamic growth and jobs, be it at the level of the EU in the context of the Lisbon Agenda, be it at the level of the WTO at the world level. Having said that, structural reforms and liberalization may also affect current account balances, but it should be clear that the mechanisms at work are complex and by no means unambiguous with respect to the effects to be expected.

The impact of structural reforms on international current account balances depends on three key factors:

* the type of reforms,
* the time horizon and
* whether the reforms mainly affect the tradable or non-tradable sector.

With respect to the first two aspects an OECD study (Kennedy and Sløk, 2005) argues that reforms of product and financial markets may imply a worsening of the current account over the medium term, whereas labour market reforms might possibly have the opposite effect. In particular, the OECD study argues that product market reforms should increase the income elasticity of demand for imports, which will tend to worsen the current account, at least in the medium term. Financial market reforms tend to stimulate the inflow of foreign capital, thereby also weakening the current account. Equilibrium can be restored if capital inflows improve productivity, and hence competitiveness in the long run.

Conversely, labour market reforms primarily have an impact on the effective labour supply, thereby reducing wages and prices in the medium term while improving the profitability of domestic capital in the long run. Labour market reforms would thus tend to improve current accounts in the short and medium term because of the improved international competitiveness of the tradable sectors.

Moreover and as pointed out by Obstfeld and Rogoff (2004), a welcome increase in the productivity of the EU would help to adjust the U.S. current account deficit only if it were to occur primarily in the non-tradable sector. If structural reforms induce a significant productivity improvement in the tradable sector, then current account positions may improve as exports become more competitive and imports less competitive. The policy implication is that structural reforms in Europe and Japan will contribute to a reduction in the US trade deficit only if, in relative terms, productivity increases in the tradable sector in the United States and in the non-tradable sector in the euro-area and Japan. Most European countries, and in particular the euro-area, have a current account that is in balance or even have a small current account surplus, which is fully in line with Europe's economic fundamentals of having a relatively wealthy and ageing economy. Further progress with structural reform in the euro-area is desirable in its own right, as it will have a beneficial effect on economic growth and resilience to shocks in Europe. Whether and to what extent structural reforms would affect the current account is far from clear and, in my view, also not a first priority.

The Euro-area as a stability anchor

EMU and the euro are an anchor for stability for neighbouring regions. A more detailed analysis shows that the euro has become particularly important as a unit of account in international goods and service trade not only in the New Member States but also in other Eastern European, Central Asian and African countries. The trade orientation of many of these countries and their desire to anchor inflation expectations has led to the euro playing a vital role in the monetary policy and exchange rate strategies of these countries. Even if the euro is not a formal or informal intermediate target, it serves as an important monetary policy indicator affecting, e.g., overall monetary conditions. Thus, the zone of stability of the euro-area is extended to other countries – within the ERM2, within the EU and beyond.

The euro also provides an anchor of stability to the international community. The ECB's mandate to focus on price stability and credibility increases the euro's attractiveness for central banks to diversify parts of their foreign reserve holdings into euro-denominated assets. The euro forms one of the main component of the Russian and Chinese reference basket. According to IMF figures, the euro captures about 25 per cent of foreign reserve assets, although many important foreign reserve accumulators are not covered by the IMF statistics. As an intervention currency, the euro naturally features very prominently in some of the New Member States. It should be noted though, that the Eurosystem does not actively promote the international use of the euro but sees this process as entirely market-driven.

Conclusion

Economic theory and practical experience demonstrate that regional integration can shelter member countries to a certain extent from internationally transmitted shocks because of the risk-sharing and consumption-smoothing properties of regional integration. A regional monetary arrangement seems to be superior in this respect to a free trade arrangement.

It is evident from the OCA literature, that a high degree of business cycle correlation within a currency area is certainly of advantage. It is also quite obvious that the degree of economic development within a unified currency area should be fairly homogeneous, since significant differences in economic development and economic growth cannot be adjusted through exchange rate fluctuations or devaluations any longer. However, as the more recent extensions to the literature have shown, optimal currency conditions are endogenous and can be shaped by economic policy and by the formation of a currency union itself. In particular, structural policies should aim at making markets more flexible such that they can cushion asymmetric shocks – which will always occur – more effectively without the need for government interference. This need for market flexibility extends to goods, labour and capital markets. Therefore structural reforms and in particular the Lisbon Agenda are so important for EMU. As a second line of defence against asymmetric shocks, national fiscal policies can play a useful role. For this to happen, they need to be in good shape in the first place. Therefore, the Maastricht fiscal convergence criteria, the Stability and Growth Pact and its aim of structurally balanced budgets are central.

The EU's single-market program, the formation of the euro-area and the structural reforms undertaken under the Lisbon Agenda are important and useful in their own respect and for Europe. They do have positive repercussions on other countries, for instance by extending the area of monetary and financial stability in which foreign exporters can do business or to which foreign governments can orient their monetary and exchange rate policies. They may also affect current account developments, but these effects are complex, hard to predict and are thus by themselves hardly suitable to motivate any specific course of action of European policies. By combining stability-oriented and sustainable macroeconomic policies with structural reforms aimed at increasing European potential growth and employment, Europe makes its best possible contribution to the development of a prosperous world economy.

Bibliography

Balassa, B. (1962) *The Theory of Economic Integration*, London: Allen and Unwin.

Bernanke, B. (2005), 'The Global Saving Glut and the U.S. Current Account Deficit', speech at the Sandridge Lecture, Virginia Association of Economics, Richmond, Virginia.

Christl, J. (2003), 'Why We Need Fiscal Rules in a Monetary Union'. http://www.oenb.at/de/presse_pub/reden/re_20031113_why_we_need_fiscal_rules.

Corsetti, G. and P. Pesenti (2002), 'Self-validating Optimum Currency Areas', mimeo.

Eagel, C. and A. Rose (2002), 'Currency Union and International Integration', *Journal of Money Credit and Banking*, 34(4), pp. 1067–89.

Eichengreen, B. and Y.C. Park (2003), 'Financial Liberalization and Capital Market Integration in East Asia', mimeo.

Frankel, J.A. and A.K. Rose (1998), 'The Endogeneity of the Optimum Currency Area Criteria', *Economic Journal*, 108:449, pp. 1009–25.

Kalemli-Ozcan, Sebnem and Bent E. Sorensen and Oved Yosha (2003), 'Risk Sharing and Industrial Specialization: Regional and International Evidence', *American Economic Review*, 93(3), pp. 903–918.

Kenen, P. (1969), 'The Theory of Optimum Currency Areas: An Eclectic View', in R. Mundell and A. Swoboda (eds.), *Monetary Problems of the International Economy*. Chicago: University of Chicago Press.

Kennedy, M. and T. Sløk (2005), 'Structural policy reforms and external imbalances', OECD Economics Department Working Paper 415.

Krugman, P. (1993), 'Lessons from Massachusetts for EMU' in F. Torres and F. Giavazzi (eds.), *Adjustment and Growth in the European Monetary Union*. Cambridge: Cambridge University Press.

McKinnon, R. (1963), 'Optimum Currency Areas', *American Economic Review*, 53, pp. 717–725.

Mundell, R.A. (1961), 'A Theory of Optimum Currency Areas', *The American Economic Review*, 51: 4 (September 1961), pp. 657–665.

Mundell, R.A. (1973), 'Uncommon Arguments for Common Currencies', in H. Johnson and A. Swoboda (eds.), *The Economics of Common Currencies*. London: Allen and Unwin.

Obstfeld, M. and K. Rogoff (2004), 'The Unsustainable US Current Account Position Revisited', Working Paper 10869, NBER. Leerseite.

5 Global imbalances and East Asia's policy adjustments

Yung Chul Park

Reserve holdings and current account imbalances in East Asia: developments in 2005

At the end of September 2005, a total of reserves held by ten East Asian economies[1] stood at $2485 billion, up from a little over 1 trillion five years earlier (see Table 5.1). The reserve increase has been the result of sterilizing the bulk of the surpluses on the current as well as capital account. These economies have been piling up since 1999. All of the ten economies have been running sizeable amounts of current account surpluses (Table 5.2). On top of these imbalances some of East Asia's emerging economies, notably China, saw swelling of capital inflows, causing a sharp increase in their capital account surpluses as well.

Much of East Asia's trade surplus has come from its trade with the US. Since 2000 the ten economies have been the source of more than 45 percent on average of the US trade deficit, which has become a major constituent of global imbalances (Table 5.3).

In 2004, the ten economies added $506.5 billion to their combined reserves after amassing $435.6 billion a year earlier (Table 5.4). In contrast, however, their reserve buildup in 2005 took a plunge to around $240 billion, less than a half of the level of 2004. There were several causes of the decrease in reserve accumulation in 2005. One was the overall drop of the current account surplus as a proportion of GDP throughout the region except in China, Hong Kong, and Singapore largely due to a steep rise in oil prices together with a slowdown in export earnings in the first half of the year. In particular, non-oil producing economies such as South Korea and Taiwan saw a sharp increase in their import bills, which cut into their surpluses, lowering the current account–GDP ratio of the two economies to 2.5 percent in 2005 from 4.7 percent in 2004.

Despite the negative effects of the oil price increase, the ten economies managed to register a surplus of $360 billion on their combined current account in 2005, which was almost same as the volume a year before.

Table 5.1 International reserves of East Asia, 1999–2005 (US dollars, billions)

	1999	2000	2001	2002	2003	2004	2005*
Japan	287.0	354.9	395.2	461.3	663.3	833.9	843.6
	(31.8)**	(34.9)	(35.1)	(34.3)	(37.2)	(36.4)	(33.9)
China	157.8	168.3	215.7	291.2	408.2	614.5	769.0
	(17.5)	(16.6)	(19.2)	(21.6)	(22.9)	(26.9)	(30.9)
Subtotal	444.8	523.2	610.9	752.5	1071.5	1448.4	1612.6
							(64.8)
Hong Kong	96.3	107.5	111.2	111.9	118.4	123.5	122.3
	(10.7)	(10.6)	(9.9)	(8.3)	(6.6)	(5.4)	(4.9)
Korea, South	74.0	96.1	102.8	121.4	155.3	199.0	206.7
	(8.2)	(9.5)	(9.1)	(9.0)	(8.7)	(8.7)	(8.3)
Singapore	76.9	80.1	75.4	82.1	95.7	112.2	115.6
	(8.5)	(7.9)	(6.7)	(6.1)	(5.4)	(4.9)	(4.7)
Taiwan	106.2	106.7	122.2	161.7	206.6	242.0	253.8
	(11.8)	(10.5)	(10.9)	(12.0)	(11.6)	(10.6)	(10.2)
Subtotal	353.4	390.6	411.6	477.1	576.0	676.7	698.4
							(28.1)
Indonesia	26.5	28.5	27.3	31.0	35.0	35.0	30.2
	(2.9)	(2.8)	(2.4)	(2.3)	(2.0)	(1.5)	(1.2)
Malaysia	30.6	29.5	30.5	34.2	44.5	66.4	79.7
	(3.4)	(2.9)	(2.7)	(2.5)	(2.5)	(2.9)	(3.2)
Philippines	13.2	13.1	13.4	13.1	13.5	12.9	16.0
	(1.5)	(1.3)	(1.2)	(1.0)	(0.8)	(0.6)	(0.6)
Thailand	34.1	32.0	32.4	38.1	41.1	48.7	48.5
	(3.8)	(3.1)	(2.9)	(2.8)	(2.3)	(2.1)	(2.0)
Subtotal	104.4	103.1	103.6	116.4	134.1	163.0	174.4
							(7)
Total	902.6	1016.9	1126.1	1346.0	1781.6	2288.1	2485.4

Source: IMF, International Financial Statistics and The Economist (2005), November 5–11 and 12–18.

Note: * At the end of September
** Percentage of the total

Although reliable data are not available this slowdown with the ballooning of the US trade deficit means that some of the global imbalances have been redistributed to oil producing economies from East Asia.

A second was the marked increase in capital outflows from Japan, Hong Kong, and Singapore. As a result of the capital outflows, Japan added only $10 billion and Hong Kong and Singapore collectively a mere $2.7 billion to their reserves in 2005 compared to a combined increase of $200 billion in the preceding year. Low interest rates in domestic capital markets and strengthening of the US dollar appear to have triggered such a large exodus of capital out of these economies. A third cause of the fall in East Asia's reserve accumulation was a large decline in capital inflows to China.

Table 5.2 Current account surpluses of ten East Asian economies (US dollar, billions)

	2000	2001	2002	2003	2004	2005* Est.	2006 Fore cast	Sum
Japan	119.7	87.8	112.4	136.2	172.1	153.0		781.2
	(56.0)**	(49.0)	(47.4)	(45.3)	(48.3)	(42.6)		(47.4)
	(2.5)***	(2.1)	(2.8)	(3.2)	(3.7)	(3.3)	(3.1)	
China	20.5	17.4	35.4	45.9	68.7	100.3		288.2
	(9.6)	(9.7)	(14.9	(15.3)	(19.3)	(27.9)		(17.5)
	(1.9)	(1.5)	2.8)	(3.2)	(4.2)	(5.5)	(4.0)	
Korea &	21.2	26.2	31.0	41.6	46.3	28.4		194.7
Taiwan	(9.9)	(14.6)	(13.1)	(13.8)	(13.0)	(7.9)		(11.8)
	(2.6)	(3.4)	(3.7)	(4.6)	(4.7)	(2.5)		
Hong Kong &	20.3	26.0	31.5	44.9	42.1	55.5		220.3
Singapore	(9.5)	(14.5)	(13.3)	(14.9)	(11.8)	(15.5)		(13.4)
	(7.9)	(10.5)	(12.7)	(18.1)	(15.6)	(19.0)		
ASEAN 4	32.1	21.7	26.7	32.2	27.3	22.0		162.0
	(15.0)	(12.1)	(11.3)	(10.7)	(7.7)	(6.1)		(9.8)
	(7.1)	(4.9)	(5.4)	(5.7)	(4.4)	(3.2)		
Total	213.8	179.1	237.0	300.8	356.5	359.2		1646.40

Note: * Estimates based on country sources and *Quarterly Review and Outlook 2005*, Global Insight
** Percent of the total
*** Percent of GDP

During the 2003–2004 period, China received more than one third of the capital inflows to emerging Asia. In 2005, capital inflows slowed to $93.4 billion compared to $138 billion a year before.

Sterilization of surpluses originating in both the current and capital accounts has kept most East Asian currencies undervalued.[2] The operation has incurred a relatively high cost.[3] By any measure of adequacy, East Asia's foreign exchange reserve has been excessive. If they are holding more reserves than they need for self-insurance and other purposes, one might ask why the East Asian economies would resist macroeconomic policy adjustments including a currency appreciation to scale down their current account surpluses and reserve accumulation. One answer is the growing doubt that neither appreciation nor expansionary monetary and fiscal policy may be effective in reducing their current account surpluses relative to global imbalances. According to the IMF report (2005), a further appreciation of East Asia's currencies 'will only have limited effect on current account positions' (p.5). The report goes on to say that domestic demand expansion will need to be driven by structural reform because there is little room for activist macroeconomic policy.

Table 5.3 Bilateral trade balances of US with East Asian economies, 2000–2005 (US dollars, millions)

	2000	2001	2002	2003	2004	2005*	Sum
Japan	-81,555.0	-69,021.6	-69,979.4	-66,032.4	-75,562.1	-68,603.5	-430,754.0
	(35.5)**	(33.5)	(30.5)	(27.0)	(25.4)	(23.9)	(28.8)
China	-83,833.0	-83,096.1	-103,064.0	-124,068.0	-161,938.0	-166,835.0	-722,835.6
	(36.5)	(40.3)	(44.9)	(50.8)	(54.3)	(58.2)	(48.4)
Hong Kong	3,133.0	4,381.4	3,266.2	4,669.3	6,513.5	6,237.8	28,201.2
	(-1.4)	(-2.1)	(-1.4)	(-1.9)	(-2.2)	(-2.2)	(-1.9)
Korea	-12,477.7	-13,000.8	-12,996.0	-13,156.8	-19,755.5	-13,158.2	-84,545.0
	(5.4)	(6.3)	(5.7)	(5.4)	(6.6)	(4.6)	(5.7)
Singapore	-1,372.0	2,651.8	1,415.5	1,422.4	4,238.1	4,935.5	13,291.3
	(0.6)	(-1.3)	(-0.6)	(-0.6)	(-1.4)	(-1.7)	(-0.9)
Taiwan	-16,096.7	-15,252.6	-13,766.2	-14,151.5	-12,879.2	-10,308.7	-82,454.9
	(7.0)	(7.4)	(6.0)	(5.8)	(4.3)	(3.6)	(5.5)
Indonesia	-7,965.2	-7,583.0	-7,087.6	-6,998.7	-8,139.1	-7,517.0	-45,290.6
	(3.5)	(3.7)	(3.1)	(2.9)	(2.7)	(2.6)	(3.0)
Malaysia	-14,630.9	-12,982.6	-13,665.3	-14,526.1	-17,257.6	-19,077.8	-92,140.3
	(6.4)	(6.3)	(6.0)	(5.9)	(5.8)	(6.7)	(6.2)
Philippines	-5,135.5	-3,665.5	-3,703.7	-2,071.7	-2,049.7	-2,071.4	-18,697.5
	(2.2)	(1.8)	(1.6)	(0.8)	(0.7)	(0.7)	(1.3)
Thailand	-9,768.1	-8,737.6	-9,932.7	-9,343.2	-11,210.5	-10,361.2	-59,353.3
	(4.3)	(4.2)	(4.3)	(3.8)	(3.8)	(3.6)	(4.0)
Total	-229,701.1	-206,306.6	-229,514.1	-244,256.9	-298,067.1	-286,759.9	-1,494,605.7
	(49.3)***	(45.9)	(45.1)	(42.0)	(42.0)	(47.9)	

Source: US Census Bureau.

Note: * Up to October
** Percentage of the total
*** Percentage of East Asia in total US trade balance

Table 5.4 Reserve buildup, 2000–2005 (US dollars, billions)

	2000	2001	2002	2003	2004	2005*	Sum
Japan	67.5	40.3	66.1	202.0	170.6	9.7	556.2
	(59.4) **	(36.8)	(30.1)	(46.4)	(33.7)	(4.0)	(34.2)
China	10.5	47.4	75.5	117.0	206.3	193.7	650.4
	(9.2)	(43.3)	(34.3)	(26.8)	(40.7)	(79.7)	(39.9)
Korea &	22.6	22.2	58.1	78.8	79.1	21.0	281.8
Taiwan	(19.9)	(20.3)	(26.4)	(18.1)	(15.6)	(8.6)	(17.3)
Hong Kong &	14.4	−1.0	7.4	20.1	21.6	2.7	65.2
Singapore	(12.7)	(−0.9)	(3.4)	(4.6)	(4.3)	(1.1)	(4.0)
ASEAN 4***	−1.3	0.5	12.8	17.7	28.9	16.0	74.6
	(−1.2)	(0.5)	(5.8)	(4.1)	(5.7)	(6.6)	(4.6)
Total	113.7	109.4	219.9	435.6	506.5	243.1	1628.2

Source: IMF, International Financial Statistics and The Economist (2005), November 5–11 and 12–18.

Note: * Estimates based on country sources and *Quarterly Review and Outlook, 2005*, Global Insight
** Percent of the total
*** Indonesia, Malaysia, the Philippines, and Thailand

It is true that many East Asian countries including China have long way to go before completing the much needed institutional reform and integration into the global financial and trade system. However, it may be also true that not much is known as to whether, how much, and over what time span, the institutional reform will contribute to eliminating the imbalance. Even if it can significantly, the reform will be a long-term process. The global economy can hardly wait for the completion of the reform. East Asia, including Japan, appears to be entering the expansionary phase of the business cycle, but given the region's export-oriented bias and high saving propensity, the prospective boom may not necessarily dissipate the gravity of the transpacific imbalance.

Among the ten economies, the two large countries – Japan and China – hold 65 percent of the region's total reserves. In 2005, they accounted for more than 70 percent of the region's current account surplus. It is therefore clear that as long as Japan and China remain unable to bring down their surpluses, other smaller East Asian countries individually or collectively could do so much to halt a further increase in the transpacific imbalance by augmenting domestic demand, simply because the number of the economies which could reflate domestic demand is small and their combined size is also small.

Recovery in Japan

There is little disagreement that East Asia as a whole will need to embrace a more domestic demand-based growth strategy to deflect the tension caused by the growing transpacific imbalance. Unless Japan is prepared to absorb more goods and services not only from the US but also from other East Asian countries, the external pressure on the rest of East Asia to expand domestic demand will not be heeded. If Japan makes headway in reviving domestic economy, other East Asian counties will find it easier to cooperate with Japan and the US to make appropriate policy adjustments needed for the resolution of the imbalance. In the absence of Japan's recovery, one cannot have much hope for restoring balance between the two sides of the Pacific with only policy changes in the rest of East Asia.

Fortunately, there is every indication that Japan is recovering. Recent forecasts show that Japan is emerging from a decade-long deflation. Industrial production rose for a fourth month in November 2005. In the same month consumer prices excluding fresh food (core price index) rose 0.1 percent from a year earlier for the first time in ten years. The Bank of Japan's Tankan survey published on December 14 shows that an index of confidence among large manufactures climbed to the highest in 2005, indicating that the pace of investment of these producers would exceed earlier expectations.

Recovery was powered by exports riding on the back of China's spectacular economic growth in 2004. After a setback in the first half of 2005, exports have been rising again at an unexpectedly strong pace, fueling corporate profits and investment. Exports appear to have bottomed out against the backdrop of recovery of imports of China. The yen is weakening in real effective term more than expected (see Figure 5.1A). Unlike in

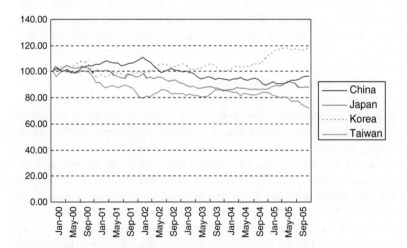

Figure 5.1A Real effective exchange rate (January 2000=100).
Source: Bank for International Settlement.

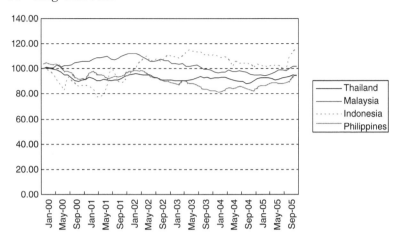

Figure 5.1B Real effective exchange rate (ASEAN 4) (January 2000=100).
Source: Bank for International Settlement.

previous periods of expansion, macroeconomic forecasts show that this time the export growth will lead to the creation of a virtuous cycle linking it with revival of investment with consumption demand. Domestic demand is therefore beginning to combine with exports to drive economic recovery.

Assuming crude oil prices are settling down, Japan is likely to enter the uprising phase of the business cycle where a sustainable recovery would help core prices register stable gains. The optimistic outlook does not necessarily mean that Japan will return to the roaring 1980s anytime soon. Many forecasters estimate that the GDP growth rate in 2005 will be 2.4 percent, lower than that in 2004, and fall off again below 2 percent for the next five years. However, recent developments lead one to believe that these forecasts are on the low side; there is little doubt that for the first time in ten years Japan's motor of domestic demand has begun humming.

Looking into the near future, despite the expected increase in consumption spending, national savings are expected to remain at around 25 percent of GDP. Household savings had slid to a little over 6 percent of GDP before turning up again in 2002. As in other East Asian economies including China, Korea, and Taiwan, the business sector has been generating large surpluses in Japan. With the recovery gathering force, Japanese households may start saving relatively more than before. The current account development will therefore hinge on investment spending. Several forecasts (see Daiwa 2005) show that there will be a marginal increase in the share of investment in GDP. As a result, compared to the 2005 level, the current account surplus will decline by 0.2 percentage points to 3 percent of GDP in 2006. Japan will therefore continue to be the major source of East Asia's current account surplus.

Nevertheless, at this stage few would argue for an activist macroeconomic policy: a right macroeconomic policy mix does not dictate more government spending for investment in infrastructure and other public projects. Japan is faced with a difficult task of managing a national debt which is approaching 150 percent of GDP, and fiscal policy has demonstratively been ineffective in turning around the economy from the decade-long stagnation. Now that the economy shows signs of recovery little change is expected in Japan's fiscal policy.

The signs of deflation ending have opened a debate whether Japan's central bank should move to end its super easy monetary policy known as quantitative easing, which has driven the real interest rate below zero. Given the moderate pace of recovery, however, there is the concern that any increase in the interest rate for restoring normalcy of monetary policy has the danger of stifling growth and plunging the economy back into recession.

The yen has weakened considerably against the US dollar in recent periods. As a result of this weakness and the deflationary trend, over the three-year period beginning in 2003, the yen has depreciated in real effective term by almost 15 percent in contrast to a large appreciation of the Korean won and strengthening of the renminbi (see Figure 5.1A). The yen's depreciation has complicated exchange rate policy in other East Asian economies. If a further appreciation of East Asian currencies is to be engineered as part of the resolution of global imbalances, then the yen's depreciation, whatever its causes may be, will have to be reversed. With core prices rising again, Japanese policymakers may find room for a stronger yen, which is a precondition for collective appreciation of East Asian currencies.

Policy adjustments in China

China's remarkable growth and entry into the global trading system have led to the creation of a triangular trade relationship involving China, the US, and Japan plus East Asia's emerging economies. In this relationship, Japan and East Asia's emerging economies export capital goods and intermediate inputs to China. China in turn uses these capital and other intermediate goods to produce a wide variety of manufactured goods that are exported to the US, EU, and other regions. One implication of this vertical integration in production is that China holds the key to the exchange rate adjustment in East Asia.

China has revalued its currency – renminbi – by 2 percent against the US dollar on 21st July in an effort to diffuse the growing external pressure for reducing its burgeoning current account surplus from the US and other countries.

Together with the initial revaluation China introduced a managed floating against a basket of major currencies and was expected to adjust the renminbi–US dollar exchange rate with changes in the bilateral exchange rates of the currencies in the basket. After five months of the operation of the new system, little is known, however, as to the currencies included in the basket or the size of the band within which the renminbi is allowed to change.

The Chinese authorities have managed the new exchange regime to strengthen further the renminbi relative to other major currencies, but the size of the appreciation has been small. Although the external pressure for additional revaluation has not subsided, it appears highly unlikely that China will accept the demand of 20 to 30 percent revaluation relative to the dollar the US administration and a number of American economists including Bergsten and Roubuni are calling for. As shown in Figure 5.3A, the renminbi–US dollar exchange rate has fluctuated within a very small band, indicating China continues to peg its currency to the US dollar. Although the renminbi has appreciated by 6 percent in real effective terms in 2005, the forward premium has been a measurable size (see Figure 5.3A).

In view of China's growing current account surplus, should the country not allow a greater flexibility of the Renminbi to let it appreciate vis-à-vis the US dollar and other currencies? Recent studies cast some doubt whether China's unilateral appreciation will have any significant impact on the aggregate current account position of the ten East Asian countries. The IMF report (2005) examines two scenarios of the renminbi appreciation. In the first scenario where China revalues its currency by 10 percent against all other currencies, Asia's current account balance, which includes India, declines by 0.1 percent of GDP in the first round and much less when multiplier effects are taken into account. The second scenario assumes that other Asian currencies also appreciate by 5 percent against non-Asian currencies. This scenario understandably produces a larger decline in Asia's current account balance up to 0.33 percent of GDP.

This small effect is in a large measure caused by the supply of goods and services in the tradable sector that appears to be highly price elastic as a result of the abundance of labor, a rapidly growing stock of capital, and improvement in productivity (Xiao and Tu 2005). China's national saving rose to 51 percent of GDP and is expected to increase further. When this high propensity to save is combined with the export led development strategy, it is likely to lower price elasticities of trade and to produce a surplus on the current account. Furthermore, after a spurt in 2004, CPI inflation has decelerated, and there is growing concern that China may become susceptible to deflation (Figure 5.2A).

While acknowledging the need to increase flexibility of the renminbi–US dollar exchange rate, the Chinese policymakers have shown strong reservations

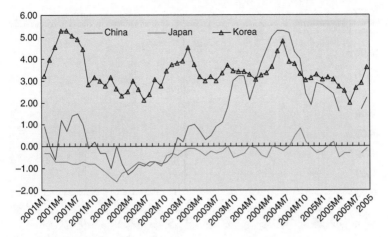

Figure 5.2A CPI Inflation: China, Japan, Korea year-on-year change.
Source: IMF, International Monetary Fund.

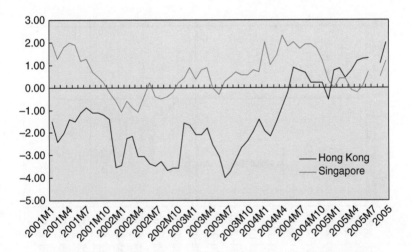

Figure 5.2B CPI Inflation: Hong Kong and Singapore year-on-year change.
Source: IMF, International Monetary Fund.

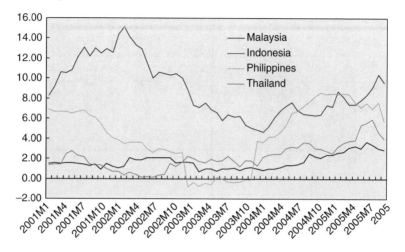

Figure 5.2C CPI Inflation: Malaysia, Indonesia, the Philippines, and Thailand year-on-year change.
Source: IMF, International Monetary Fund.

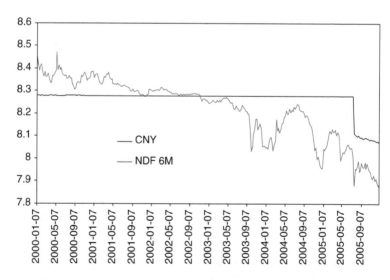

Figure 5.3A Nominal exchange rate and NDF forward (6 months) in China.
Source: Bloomberg.

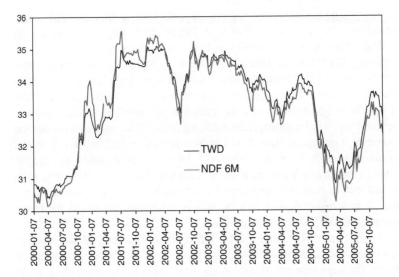

Figure 5.3B Nominal exchange rate and NDF forward (6 months) in Taiwan.
Source: Bloomberg.

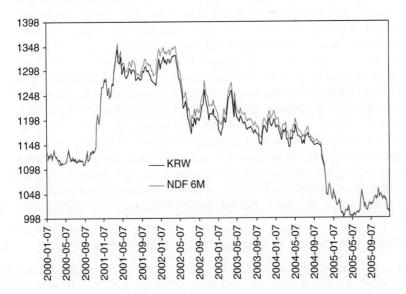

Figure 5.3C Nominal exchange rate and NDF forward (6 months) in Korea.
Source: Bloomberg.

about making an initial move at present with the fear that the small move could exacerbate capital inflows. A larger move may be necessary to restrain speculative capital inflows, but such a policy change has not been seriously contemplated because its negative impact on employment and growth and on the banking sector saddled with large amounts of non-performing loans. It may be true that there is little persuasive evidence that a unilateral appreciation will be effective in curtailing China's current account surplus. However, if the Chinese authorities continue to delay the currency adjustment, then it will induce further capital inflows with the consequences more serious than the loss of employment and output. China's currency adjustment is desirable and in the interest of the region as it will lead to more balanced growth of the tradable and non-tradable sector and from a regional point of view will help facilitate an across the board appreciation of East Asian currencies.

As for macroeconomic policy management, looking at the size of government debt or fiscal balance as a percentage of GDP, China has ample room for expansionary fiscal policy (see Table 5.5), although it is an entirely different matter whether it has the administrative capacity required to conduct an efficient tax and expenditure policy. On the front of monetary policy, China's tightly managed exchange rate system allows scope for an independent domestic interest rate policy given porous but substantial and effective controls on international capital movements. Indeed, to prevent overheating of the economy and financial instability, the Chinese authorities have adopted both administrative measures and interest rate rises to rein in the rapid growth of credit and capital investment. These measures have achieved some success in stabilizing the rate of inflation. Despite the tightening of credit growth, the rate of growth of money supply has accelerated in recent periods and hence there is still large excess liquidity in the system, which continues to fuel real estate speculation and asset price inflation. In view of these developments, a loosening of China's credit policy to permit more rapid growth of investment in order to restrain the current account surplus would run the risk of overheating the economy and exacerbating the non-performing loans problems at the banks as excessive investments may result in a large increase in business failures (Genberg *et al.*, 2005).

Policy adjustments in East Asia's emerging economies

Current account balances of South Korea and Taiwan fell to 2 and 3.2 percent of GDP in 2004, respectively, and this trend is expected to continue into 2006. Domestic demand has been growing at a somewhat higher rate than before, although export earnings will continue to drive economic expansion in 2006 in both economies, despite the sharp appreciation of the Korean

Table 5.5 Selected fiscal indicators (In percent of GDP)

	General Government Gross Debt						Central Govermental Fiscal Balance					
	2000	2001	2002	2003	2004 Est.	2005 Proj.	2000	2001	2002	2003	2004 Est.	2005 Proj.
Japan	139.3	148.8	158.4	164.7	169.2	174.4	−6.9	−6.3	−6.9	−7.1	−7.0	−6.9
China	16.9	18.7	20.6	21.3	20.0	19.1	−3.6	−3.1	−3.3	−2.8	−1.7	−1.7
Hong Kong							−0.6	−5.0	−4.9	−3.2	−0.8	−0.7
South Korea	29.2	33.8	32.4	32.6	33.6	32.9	1.1	0.6	2.3	2.7	2.3	2.2
Singapore							7.9	4.8	4	5.8	3.9	4.5
Taiwan	24.4	31.5	35.1	37.6	39.6	41.5	−0.5	−2.8	−4.3	−4.0	−3.3	−3.0
Indonesia	91.3	78.2	69.2	60.2	57.9	53.3	−3.4	−3.2	−1.5	−1.9	−1.4	−1.6
Malaysia	36.7	43.6	45.6	47.1	46	44.8	−5.7	−5.5	−5.6	−5.3	−4.3	−3.5
Philippines	89.1	88.4	93.8	101.3	99.6	97.0	−4.6	−4.6	−5.6	−5.0	−4.2	−3.9
Thailand	23	24.8	31.3	28.5	28.6	26.2	−2.0	−2.1	−2.3	0.4	0.3	0.5

Source: Regional Outlook September 2005, Asia and Pacific Department, IMF.

won in recent periods. As a regional financial center with an open trade regime and capital markets Hong Kong and Singapore have seldom been identified as sources of global imbalances. Although their current account balances as a proportion of GDP have been large and growing, they have mostly been balanced out by large capital outflows.

Among ASEAN 4, Thailand recorded a deficit on its current account in 2005. Indonesia and the Philippines have been battling for subduing inflationary pressures (Figure 5.2C). Given the small size of their current account surpluses, these countries do not figure importantly in the resolution of global imbalances. Malaysia is the only country that has continuously run sizeable amounts of surplus on its current account, which has averaged more than 13 percent of GDP since 2003. It appears that there will be no appreciable change in Malaysia's current account imbalance for the next two years. Therefore, among East Asia's eight emerging economies, Malaysia, South Korea, and Taiwan may need to make policy adjustments as part of East Asia's efforts to resolve global imbalances.

Fiscal policy

East Asian countries have traditionally valued fiscal prudence highly, and with the IMF on the watch many of them have not seriously considered fiscal expansion as a means of stimulating domestic demand regardless of its effectiveness since the 1997–1998 crisis. Reflecting this fiscal conservatism, the government debt as a proportion of GDP has been low in East Asia except for Japan and the Philippines (Table 5.5). Many young democracies in East Asia suffer from the rigidity of and lag in fiscal policy as a result of a slow and complicated political process of determining the size and distribution of government expenditure between projects, sectors, and regions. Fiscal policy can be pro cyclical if the lag is long and persistent. East Asian policymakers are also aware of the possibility of replicating Japan's experience with a pump-priming policy that has resulted mostly in a massive increase in national debt.

Among the ASEAN states, Indonesia and the Philippines are currently in no position to contemplate any further increase in government spending or cut taxes. The Indonesian government is committed to further fiscal consolidation to reduce vulnerability arising from the high level of public debt. Its objective is to achieve broad budgetary balance by 2006–2007 consistent with lowering public debt to below 50 percent of GDP. The Indonesian government has also been engaged in fiscal reform that envisages more efficient tax administration and improvement in budget preparation and execution. The size of the public debt in the Philippines has been close to 100 percent of GDP, which is high and unsustainable. The government has committed itself to balancing the budget by 2009 by tax increases and streamlining fiscal expenditure.

Thailand and Malaysia have been able to bring down budgetary deficits to a manageable level, and as such they do not have either budgetary deficit or national debt problems that could rule out an expansionary fiscal policy. Thailand has a room for additional fiscal stimulus, and its authorities have seen the need to run a budgetary deficit to boost domestic demand. South Korea, Singapore, and Taiwan could certainly take high doses of fiscal expansion. Of theses countries, South Korea has been most active in implementing an expenditure switching policy by combining an increase in government spending with an exchange rate appreciation. The two other countries have not been as active as export earnings have been large enough to sustain relatively high rates of growth.

Monetary policy

Monetary policy in East Asia is accommodating as judged by the level of real short-term interest rates. Since the financial crisis of 1997–1998 real interest rates have declined in most economies and they are now close to zero and even negative in some cases. (Table 5.6). Would it be appropriate for monetary policy to be even more expansionary for the purpose of contributing to the reduction of external imbalances? For a number of reasons, it may not. The responsiveness of corporate investment in Asia to short-term interest rates appears to be very low. The corporate sector is producing a financial surplus in most countries in the region. This net corporate savings suggests that the cost of bank loans or newly issued bonds might not have a strong effect on investment demand.

Table 5.6 Short-term real interest rates

	1990–1996	1999–2001	2002–2004	2005 (Jan.– Apr.)
Hong Kong	−3.59	8.26	1.99	1.43
Philippines	4.20	4.53	1.84	−1.39
China		5.04	1.26	0.69
Indonesia	4.27	2.71	1.18	−2.95
Malaysia	2.59	1.54	0.93	0.35
Taiwan	3.05	4.47	0.76	−0.83
Korea	7.35	2.53	0.59	0.15
Japan	2.38	0.80	0.45	0.21
Thailand	4.97	2.43	0.17	−0.66
Singapore		0.36	−0.15	1.39

Note: The real interest rates have been calculated as the difference between representative short-term market interest rates and the actual CPI inflation rate over the past year.
Source: Genberg, McCauley, Park and Persaud (2005).

Indeed, the persistent sluggishness of investment demand in East Asian countries (except China) in the presence of very low real interest rates suggests that traditional channels of monetary policy, in particular the cost of capital channel, may have weakened. For example, it is generally believed that this is the case in Japan, and it may also be true in Taiwan and South Korea. At present, therefore, further easing of monetary policy would not stimulate consumption and investment demand while it runs the risk of fueling the ongoing asset inflation in the cases of China, Korea, and Thailand, and contributing to general inflationary pressures in Indonesia and the Philippines. Indeed, any additional cuts in interest rates could lead to another boom-bust cycle as in the run-up to the crisis in 1997. No country in the region is willing to take this risk.

Aside from the ineffectiveness, further easing will run into conflict with explicit or implicit domestic inflation objectives for the conduct of monetary policy in ASEAN 4 and Korea which have adopted inflation targeting. This has limited the scope of expansionary monetary policy at this stage. At the first sign of CPI inflation in 2005, the central bank of Korea raised the interest rate and Taiwan's central bank also recently hinted the possibility of raising the interest rates.

Exchange rate policy coordination in East Asia

There is little disagreement that an across the board appreciation of East Asian currencies constitutes an important component of the resolution of global imbalances. However, as noted earlier, if China insists on maintaining its limited flexibility, other East Asian countries are not likely to let their currencies appreciate vis-à-vis the renminbi as China has emerged as their export competitor in regional as well as global markets.[4]

Whatever China does, would it not be in the interest of other East Asian countries to allow their currencies strengthen relative to the US dollar independently? Apparently to many East Asian countries, it is not. If the dollar falls as it has and China maintains its near-fixed parity vis-à-vis the dollar, then other East Asian countries with an intermediate currency regime fear that they will be forced to absorb disproportionately more the pressures of appreciation on the East Asian currencies overall. That is, with the weakening of the dollar, their concern is that more of capital inflows into East Asia will flock to the countries that look vulnerable to appreciation, causing a larger appreciation of their currencies relative to the dollar than otherwise, if they do not intervene.

What is significant about China's move to an intermediate regime is that it has in theory, though not in reality necessarily, broadened the scope of coordination of exchange rate policy among some of the ten East Asia economies and revived the discussion of establishing a new modality of cooperation for monetary integration in the region. As Kawai (2002) notes, South Korea and Thailand have shifted to a de facto currency basket arrangement similar to Singapore's managed floating since the crisis. Malaysia has also adopted a basket arrangement. The behavior of real effective exchange rates of Indonesia and the Philippines (Figure 5.1B) also indicate that the currencies of the two economies are linked to a basket of major currencies. Excluding the yen, which will remain an independently floating major currency, practically all emerging economies in East Asia now have a similar framework of exchange rate policy.

Since the policy authorities of these economies with a basket arrangement are expected to adjust their dollar exchange rates with changes in the bilateral exchange rates the dollar, euro, and yen to keep their nominal or real effective exchange rates stable, ASEAN 4, China, Korea, and Taiwan will keep a close watch over changes in the dollar exchange rates of other economies just to make sure that their export competitiveness does not slip. However, in reality it is difficult to ascertain the causes of changes in the dollar exchange rates of East Asian currencies. Before the regime shift in China, a depreciation of the dollar against the yen or the euro automatically increased the competitiveness of Chinese exports. With the introduction of a basket system, such a change in competitiveness can be minimized, but China has not managed the system in a manner that was expected.

Among China, South Korea, Taiwan, and ASEAN 4, if any economy moves to weaken its currency vis-à-vis the dollar to let its nominal effective exchange rate depreciate, such an intervention will set off competitive devaluation in the region. To prevent such a disarray the competitive clash would be in the interest of the region. Clearly there is a need for a collective exchange rate policy for the entire region, and there is an institutional arrangement such as the ASEAN+3 meetings of finance ministers or their deputies, which could serve as fora for coordination of exchange rate policy among the seven of the ten economies ASEAN 4, China, Korea, and Singapore(excluding Japan, Hong Kong, and Taiwan). However, if the past experience with policy coordination among ASEAN+3 is any guide, the seven countries will not be able to agree on any issue as complicated as the realignment of their currencies vis-à-vis the dollar. There are two structural problems causing this impasse.

One problem that has frustrated exchange rate policy coordination in East Asia is that Japan is a very important trade partner to, but cannot or does not want to participate in any regional framework for exchange rate policy coordination in East Asia. This is because the yen is a free floating international currency, whereas other East Asian currencies are non-convertible (except for the Singapore dollar) and linked to baskets of regional and international currencies. Japan has a relatively small external sector, which makes it less sensitive to currency fluctuations compared with other East Asian economies including China. This means that the seven economies will have to work out a regional cooperative arrangement for exchange rate stability among themselves. Given its growing economic and political influences in East Asia, China could provide leadership for the formation of such a regional arrangement; it may be able to do so in the long-run, but not in the near future.

Another constrain on regional cooperation on collective exchange rate policy is related to the differences in bilateral trade imbalances among the East Asian countries. When the ten East Asian countries are divided into Japan, China, and the rest comprising other emerging economies, Japan has been running surpluses in its trade with all these economies including China.[5] The group of emerging economies on the other hand has been running a surplus in its trade with China, but a large deficit with Japan.

Because of these different profiles of the bilateral imbalances, the group of East Asian emerging economies may be able to accept a simultaneous appreciation of their currencies and the renminbi against the US dollar. However, if the yen is not expected to appreciate, China and other emerging economies will not go along with the joint appreciation, for fear of deepening their persistent structural trade deficits with Japan. And the yen will not necessarily appreciate vis-à-vis the US dollar unless the Japanese authorities intervene. To economists, bilateral trade imbalances may not matter, but to politicians and policymakers, they matter and a lot, especially when coordination of exchange rate policy and the source of deficits in Japan.

This dilemma together with trade integration in East Asia underscores the need to bring Japan into a regional arrangement for exchange rate policy cooperation. However, even if Japan were to be included, this would not solve the problem, because Japan and China would be unlikely to see eye to eye on many regional issues, largely because of their rivalry for a greater economic and political influence in East Asia. Even if the two were able to work together, it is questionable whether they would be able to persuade other emerging economies to agree on bilateral exchange rate adjustments, in particular if these countries had to revalue their currencies.

Prospects of reserve buildup in East Asia

A recent IMF (2005) report describes the decline in reserve accumulation in East Asia in 2005 as having been dramatic. Is this change a promising sign that East Asia's imbalance vis-à-vis the rest of the world is resolving itself into a manageable magnitude through market forces and no longer poses threat to global financial stability?

If the terms of trade improvement as the recent upsurge in crude oil prices is tempered and the US trade deficit continues to increase East Asia may start registering a larger surplus in the current account again. As growth picks up in the region on the back of Japan's recovery, some of East Asia's emerging economies may experience a surge in capital inflow as they did in 2003 and 2004.

Against these possible developments, some of East Asia's emerging economies have undertaken or are planning to initiate large public investment projects as Thailand has whereas others have loosened up control over the capital account to facilitate capital outflows. Eight years after the outbreak of the financial crisis in 1997–1998, East Asia's emerging economies excluding China appear to have eliminated much of the excess capacity they built during the boom years of the early 1990s and hence will resume their capital spending (Lee, 2006). As shown in Figure 5.1A, currencies of Korea and ASEAN 4 have appreciated in real effective term in recent periods and will continue to do so if the US dollar depreciates against the euro and the yen as many market participants expect. When these developments are taken into consideration, there is a high probability that the gap between saving and investment as a proportion of GDP will decline throughout East Asia so much so that East Asia's NIEs and ASEAN 4 are not likely to be adding to global imbalances. However, the current account surplus will continue to remain over 3 and 4 percent of GDP in Japan and China in 2006 and thereafter respectively. This means that the transpacific imbalance between East Asia as a whole and the US will be transformed into largely an imbalance between Japan and China on the one hand and the US on the other.

Notes

1 They are: China, Japan, Korea, Taiwan, Hong Kong, Indonesia, Malaysia, the Philippines, Singapore, and Thailand.
2 The reserve accumulation is a prima facie evidence of undervaluation.
3 The cost arising from the interest rate differential between the domestic and foreign interest rates has been a minor one compared to other more serious cost factors. The weaker dollar has inflicted substantial capital losses on their holdings of dollar assets. The undervalued currency along with the export-led growth strategy has discouraged investment in the non-tradable sector, causing misallocation of resources and unbalanced growth of the economy.
4 A 2004 IMF report on Indonesia reflects this gridlock when it says that in 2003 Indonesia's currency level was not seriously misaligned as it was broadly in line with other regional currencies from a competitiveness point of view.
5 According to Chinese trade statistics, China is in deficit vis-à-vis Japan. Japanese statistics, however, show that Japan is running a deficit in its trade with China. The difference stems from the inclusion of Hong Kong as part of China in the Japanese statistics.

Bibliography

Genberg, Hans, Robert McCauley, Yung Chul Park, and Avinash Persaud (2005), 'Official Reserves and Currency Management in Asia: Myth, Reality and the Future', Geneva Reports on the World Economy 7, International Center for Monetary and Banking Studies.

IMF(2005), Asia-Pacific Regional Outlook – September 2005, Asia and Pacific Department.

Kawai, M (2002), 'Exchange Rate Arrangements in East Asia: Lessons from the 1997–98 Currency Crisis', *Monetary and Economic Studies* 20, no s-1 (December), Tokyo, Bank of Japan, Institute for Monetary and Economic Studies.

Lee, Jong Wha (2006), 'Domestic Investment and Regional Imbalances in East Asia', KIEP and PRI seminar, *'Emerging Financial Risks in East Asia?'* January 12–13.

Makino, Junich (2005), *Japan's Economic Outlook*, No 147, Daiwa Institute of Research, Ltd., Tokyo, Japan.

Xiao, Geng and Zhengge Tu (2005), 'China's Industrial Productivity Revolution: A Stochastic Frontier Production Function Analysis of China's Large and Medium Industrial Enterprises during 1995–2002', WEAI and HKEA Conference, Hong Kong, January 15.

6 Global imbalances and regional monetary cooperation

Charles Wyplosz

The present current account global imbalances are usually described as pitting the US against East Asia, with Europe an innocent bystander that can be hit if things go wrong. The rest of the world is largely ignored, presumably because its size in world trade is small relative to the big three areas. Being small does not mean that the rest of the world would escape the adverse consequences of a poor unwinding of the imbalances, it means that there is little it can do to guard against such an outcome. This means that much of the discussion is about policy cooperation among the big players. The present note starts from this observation and examines what difference regional cooperation can make to global cooperation.

To start with, how much is a US vs. East Asia vs. Europe issue? The broad facts are well known. The large US current account deficit is approximately matched by the collective East Asian surplus while Europe is roughly in balance. To be complete, we need to note that it is the euro-area that is in balance while the UK has had a moderate deficit of about two per cent for the last few years. For this reason, and also because it does not belong to the euro-area, the UK is one of the large players left out of the present discussion (the others being India and Brazil).

The question then becomes whether regional cooperation could play a useful role in this instance and perhaps in other instances as well. This question can be broken into two parts: 1) Are there incentives to regional cooperation? 2) Is regional cooperation naturally helping to deal with the global imbalance?

The global and regional situation

Figure 6.1 shows the pattern of current account balances in the largest countries in East Asia and the euro-area. The figure reveals that the countries are far from homogeneous. There is about as much distance between Indonesia's small surplus and Malaysia's huge surplus as there is between

Spain's deficit and the Dutch and German surpluses. In this case at least, the incentives for common action are not particularly strong. At least, in the case of East Asia, there is a common incentive to reduce surpluses while, within the euro-area some countries may be reluctant to deepen their current account deficits. The fact that the situation differs from one country to another does not mean that coordination is hopeless, though. Coordination does not mean that all countries take the same measures. The implication, rather, is that coordination must involve assigning different policy actions to different countries. Logical as it sounds, it raises serious implementation issues.

A cooperative resolution of the current imbalance problem calls for a climbdown of the US deficit matched by a reduction of the East Asian surplus and some absorption by the European countries as well. This is the theory, but how can that be done in practice? One instrument is the exchange rate, i.e. monetary policy, the other is demand management via fiscal policy. A collective appreciation of the East Asian currencies and of the euro would be the first response. A collective fiscal expansion in East Asia and the euro-area, coupled with fiscal restriction in the US, would be the second response. The next sections look at the impact of regional cooperation on this game plan.

Incentives to regional exchange rate cooperation

In the euro-area, an exchange rate appreciation can only be collective, of course, but is the Eurosystem more likely to reach such a decision than the national central banks (NCBs) would on their own? On the one hand, the Eurosystem is probably more sensitive to global issues than the NCBs. As a global player, it is more likely to feel some degree of responsibility for world issues. It can meaningfully discuss the issue with the other parties involved, credibly commit and deliver on any agreement. In addition, any decision will apply to all member countries; thus the existing regional arrangement solves the coordination issue, removing the threat of intra-European beggar-thy-neighbor freeriding responses. In that way, it makes global cooperation more likely.

There remains the question of who controls the exchange rate, the Eurosystem or theTreasuries, i.e. the Eurogroup. It is assumed here that it is the Eurosystem, or that the Eurosystem would get the support of the Eurogroup were it to reach an exchange rate intervention agreement with the other parties. This assumption is not necessarily safe. Yet, the Eurosystem can always try to achieve the same result on its own, by independently tightening its monetary policy stance while talking the euro up. Maybe this is already underway …

Yet, some considerations lead to the opposite conclusion. To start with, the euro-area is a fairly closed economy. Not only does that mean that the effect of any exchange rate appreciation on world imbalances will be limited, it also implies that the risks associated with a non-cooperative global reaction are limited. Then comes the fact that not all EU members are in the euro-area. As a consequence there still exists a beggar-thy-neighbor problem, especially as the UK, which currently exhibits a current account deficit, is unlikely to join the Eurosystem should it decide to let the euro appreciate. Finally, are the 18 members of the Eurosystem's Council of Governors likely to back an appreciation? Note that the individual countries are in different economic situations. Some have current account deficits and some have surpluses. Those that run surpluses and could therefore support an appreciation are also characterized by weak economies. At a time when the recovery is far from solid, these countries are unlikely to welcome a loss in international competitiveness. Among the fast growing countries, Spain is increasingly concerned by its external deficit and lack of competitiveness. This is not just bad luck but, partly at least, a well-anticipated consequence of the monetary union. Fast growing countries typically face higher inflation rates and, therefore a gradual loss of competitiveness. Figure 6.2 confirms that it is indeed the case (the correlation coefficient between the current account and inflation across countries is −0.56; excluding Portugal, it is −0.81).

This is the way differences in economic conditions, a currency union's Achilles' heel, are self-stabilizing. In the present circumstances, this built-in feature works against support for an appreciation of the euro.

The situation in Asia is different in many respects. As displayed in Figure 6.1, all the major countries currently run a current account surplus. At the same time, growth rates differ quite significantly between Japan, barely out of its lost decade, and China, with a breakneck performance. As a consequence, an exchange rate appreciation is conceivable but not a uniform one. Fortunately, there is no monetary union and therefore scope for different rates of appreciation. Still, as we have seen in the recent path, this is not an easy step.

An exchange rate appreciation is likely to correct the current account surpluses but also to slow growth down. As Figure 6.3 shows, the East Asian current account surpluses are broadly similar, irrespective of the growth rate. If reducing the current account is the intention, similar reductions would be a natural objective, but countries with relatively low growth rates – this is Asia, not Europe! – will obviously be unwilling to take contractionary measures. Would China, the largest country with the biggest absolute current account deficit and the highest growth rate, be the one letting its exchange rate appreciate most? This question has been on the agenda of the G7 for nearly two years.

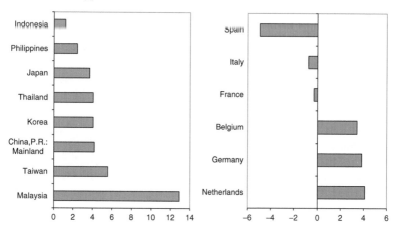

Figure 6.1 Current accounts in East Asia and Europe (% of GDP – 2004).
Source: Asian countries: International Financial Statistics, IMF; Central Bank of China (Taiwan); European countries: Economic Outlook, OECD.

Note: Malaysia's figure is for 2003.

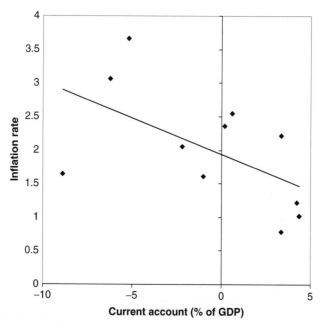

Figure 6.2 Inflation and the current account in the euro-area in 2005.
Source: Economic Outlook, OECD.

Note: Luxembourg is excluded.

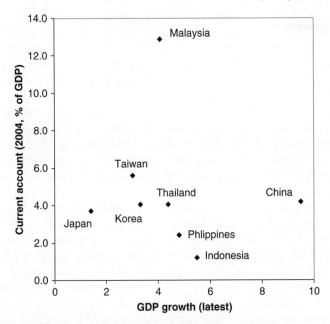

Figure 6.3 Current accounts and GDP growth rates in Asia (2004).
Source: Asian countries: International Financial Statistics, IMF; Central Bank of China (Taiwan); The Economist.

One reason why China and other East Asian countries are reacting with extreme caution is that 'export-led growth' is seen throughout the region as a winning strategy, whether it has in fact been a key success factor or not. In this view, the Asian countries, which compete against each other on both their own and foreign markets, see the exchange rate as a key strategic tool. Undervaluation is the name of the game, and they are not ready to blame each other for undervaluation. They seem to be ready to take risks with the resolution of the global imbalances rather than take risks with the 'export-led growth' strategy. Is this a flawed calculation?

To face the risk of large-scale international monetary disturbances, the East Asian countries have been accumulating huge stockpiles of foreign exchange reserves. The more threatening are the global imbalances, the more they want to run balance of payment surpluses and, therefore, the more attached they are to exchange rate undervaluation. Thus, calling upon them to help with the global imbalance makes them even less willing to let their exchange rates appreciate.

Logical as it may appear, the calculation is flawed in at least three respects. First, large stocks of foreign exchange reserves are largely illusory. Under the current circumstances worldwide exchange rate turmoil is likely to press for an appreciation of the East Asian currencies. Second, should the markets reverse their views and press for depreciation of the East Asian currencies, no stock of foreign reserves is large enough to face a determined worldwide stampede. Of course, those countries that still allow for capital controls stand a fair chance of resisting such a stampede, but that would only worsen the unwinding of the imbalances. Thus, third, the strategy designed to sustain growth could well turn against its aim by provoking a worldwide contraction that would shrink the East Asian country foreign markets.

This is where regional cooperation could make a difference. The buildup of foreign exchange reserves is seen by each East Asian country as its own insurance against an exchange rate crisis. A collective exchange rate arrangement, either in the form of the European Exchange Mechanism or a monetary union, would go a long way toward solving the exchange rate threat. Obviously, such an arrangement would not deal with the exchange rate between East Asian currencies and the dollar or the euro, but it would greatly reduce the risk of serious misalignments within the region. It would also allow a pooling of national foreign exchange reserves – an objective that several East Asian countries are now actively pursuing. A reduced need for reserves would mean less support for exchange rate overvaluation and, maybe, more willingness to cooperate with the rest of the world in dealing with the global imbalance.

The situation with fiscal policy is similar but the conclusions are radically different. What is needed is an expansionary move that would raise domestic demands and imports in Europe and East Asia, coupled with a contractionary stance in the US. There is no indication that the US is willing to entertain such an action, even though this is exactly what its budget deficit calls for. Assuming that it does, what does that imply for Europe and East Asia and regional cooperation?

The largest European countries – including the UK – already run sizeable budget deficits, and have done so for many years running, see Figure 6.4. An expansionary move, even if it were to succeed and speed up growth – would only deepen the existing deficits. There is obviously little appetite for such a move. Is cooperation likely to change that view? Presently, the only cooperation that exists in the fiscal policy area is the Stability and Growth Pact. The Pact, even in its revised form, would not condone any expansionary move in the large countries, precisely those that matter for world cooperation.

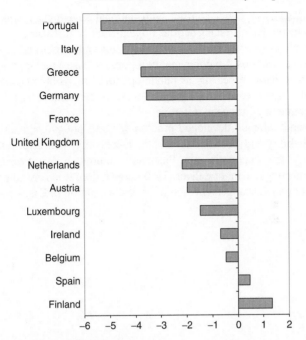

Figure 6.4 Budget balances (% of GDP – 2005).
Source: Economic Outlook, OECD.

Independently of the Pact, there is frequent talk about wider fiscal policy cooperation. Proponents envision a process whereby the Eurogroup would work toward agreeing on a euro-area-wide fiscal stance. This objective seems unlikely to be reachable for the foreseeable future. Fiscal policy is an intensely political activity as it involves national governments and parliaments. The treaties explicitly regard fiscal policy as a matter of national sovereignty. Subjecting national fiscal policies to a European constraint is unlikely to succeed until member states are willing to give up a sufficient degree of sovereignty in this area. While a systematic, year-by-year, coordination process of agreeing on a euro-area-wide fiscal policy stance is currently ruled out, occasional cooperation could be imagined. It would take exceptional circumstances for finance ministers to agree on mutual commitments and to manage to master the support of their governments and parliaments.

Are current global imbalances just such case? This is very unlikely. Dismal scenarios of the European message in G7 meetings are that both the US and Europe need to come with their budget deficits. The Stability and

Growth Pact is in direct conflict with national sovereignty. This is one reason why the Pact is facing serious implementation difficulties. Financial market meltdowns triggering worldwide exchange rate crises and depression are just that scenarios. No policymaker is going to base a major policy decision on a scenario, especially as public opinions are visibly not interested. This is already the case in the US, and US inactivity in this respect is bound to undermine any European initiative.

If Europe's already developed process of fiscal policy cooperation, the flawed Stability and Growth Pact and the increasingly cohesive Eurogroup (especially the Economic and Financial Committee that prepares the group's meetings), cannot deliver fiscal cooperation, it is hard to see what form of regional arrangement would foster cooperation in East Asia.

7 Global payments imbalances and East Asia's monetary and financial cooperation

Masahiro Kawai[1]

Introduction

Widening global payments imbalances centering on the United States have provoked debate among the international policy community, academics, and researchers. The United States has experienced rising current account deficits while East Asian economies – e.g., Japan, People's Republic of China (PRC), and other emerging economies in the region – and oil exporting countries have seen large current account surpluses. Persistent current account deficits have led to a continuous increase in US net external liabilities. With current and capital account surpluses, PRC has been accumulating sizable foreign exchange reserves under a tightly managed exchange rate regime, thereby financing an increasing portion of the US current account deficit. The heart of the debate is: whether the rising US current account deficit is sustainable or not; how and when the unwinding of global imbalances will take place if it ever occurs; how much impact this may have on the world economic and financial conditions; and what type of policy mix will be desirable to avoid disruptive adjustment – a dollar hard landing, interest rate hikes, and asset price collapse in the United States – which can have serious, negative impacts on the world economy and finance.

The gravest scenario is an abrupt and disorderly adjustment of the US dollar, accompanied by a sharp increase in long-term interest rates, a collapse of asset prices – those of bonds, shares, and houses – and a severe economic recession in the United States. US long-term interest rates have so far remained at historically low levels, providing an impetus to the real estate and housing boom. A sharp increase in long-term rates could adversely affect asset prices and consumer spending, a key driver of US economic growth in recent years. These disruptive events can exert serious impacts on the global economy and financial markets, particularly in many emerging market economies.

The paper argues that the current pace of global imbalances – if left unaddressed – is not sustainable in the long run. Both deficit and surplus countries must share the responsibility to ensure the orderly resolution of global payments imbalances. The United States needs to make the most urgent efforts to raise national savings through fiscal deficit reduction and personal saving promotion. Japan and the euro-area economies need to stimulate domestic demand and growth performance through structural reforms including fiscal consolidation. PRC and other emerging East Asian economies need to rebalance the sources of growth away from exports to domestic demand through structural policies and greater exchange rate flexibility. Oil exporting countries need to increase their domestic spending with a focus on the expansion of supply capacity of crude oil.

In addition, the paper argues that East Asia is advised to strengthen regional monetary and financial cooperation in order to both contribute to the orderly resolution of global imbalances and to prepare for possible disorderly and disruptive adjustment. Measures include: making the economic surveillance process and the reserve pooling arrangement (the Chiang Mai Initiative) more effective; advancing initiatives for Asian bond market development; and adopting greater exchange rate flexibility vis-à-vis the US dollar while maintaining intra-regional rate stability.

The organization of the paper is as follows. The second section considers recent developments of global payments imbalances, focusing on current account balances, net capital flows, foreign exchange reserve accumulation, and net international investment positions. The third section examines factors behind growing global payments imbalances from the perspective of savings and investment relationships. The fourth section explores potential problems of continuously running large global payments imbalances, focusing on the 'sustainability' of rising net external liabilities, and their implications for the US and world economy. The fifth section presents desirable policy actions, to prevent disorderly and disruptive adjustment, for both deficit and surplus countries. The sixth section recommends modalities of East Asian monetary and financial cooperation for contributing to the orderly resolution of imbalances and for cushioning the possible negative impact once disorderly adjustment becomes imminent. The seventh section provides concluding remarks.

Current accounts, capital flows, reserve accumulation, and net international investment positions

The world economy has experienced growing payments imbalances; the United States runs a large current account deficit, while East Asia and oil exporting countries run large current account surpluses. Without offsetting capital outflows – or with net capital inflows as in the case of PRC – East Asia's current account surpluses have led to a large buildup of foreign exchange reserves. These reserves held by 11 major East Asian economies – including six ASEAN members: PRC; Japan; Republic of Korea (Korea); Hong Kong,China; and Taipei,China – now add up to more than $2.5 trillion, which is 60 percent of the global foreign exchange reserves. Oil exporting countries have also emerged as a large surplus group as a result of recent hikes of crude oil prices.

Figure 7.1 summarizes current account balances of the top ten largest surplus and deficit countries. The United States clearly stands out in terms of its size of current account deficit; it is by far the largest deficit country, exceeding $800 billion in 2005. There are a few other deficit countries, such as Spain ($83 billion) and the United Kingdom ($58 billion), whose deficits are relatively large in the world but are significantly smaller than that of the United States. On the other hand, several economies run large current account surpluses, such as Japan ($164 billion), PRC ($150 billion), Germany ($112 billion), Saudi Arabia ($87 billion), and Russia ($84 billion), but the size of their individual surpluses is not quite comparable to that of

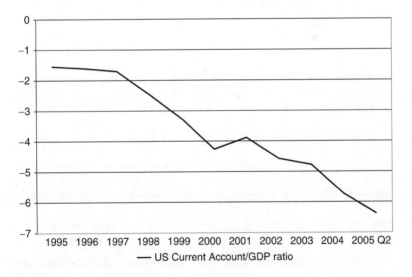

Figure 7.1 US current account balance (% of GDP).
Source: Datastream and world development indicators.

the US deficit. Germany's surpluses have largely been offset by deficits of many European countries so that the euro-area as a whole has not exhibited large and rising payments imbalances (Figure 7.2). Essentially, the global imbalance problem is primarily that of US deficits, though surpluses of East Asia and oil exporting countries – including Russia – also matter.

United States

Between 1990 and 2005, the United States ran current account deficits in all years except in 1991, and corresponding capital account surpluses throughout the period. The $805 billion in current account deficit in 2005 was $390 billion greater than the level of deficit in 2000. As a percent of US GDP, its current account deficit rose from 1.5 percent in 1995 to 4.2 percent in 2000, and to 6.5 percent in 2005. According to OECD projections, the US current account deficit in 2006 may exceed 7 percent of GDP (OECD, *Economic Outlook*, 78).

Until 2000, the US deficit was financed largely through private capital inflows in the form of foreign direct investment (FDI) and purchases of US debt securities. Beginning in 2001, however, this changed as the United States saw a decline in FDI inflows and even a net outflow of FDI,

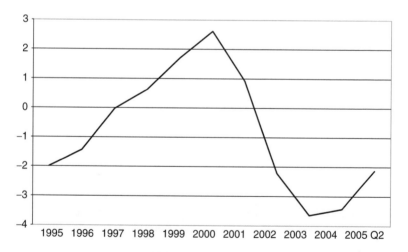

Figure 7.2 US fiscal surplus/GDP (%).
Source: Datastream and world development indicators.

and most of its current account deficit began to be financed by capital inflows through debt securities. Though FDI registered a net inflow once again in 2005, the current account deficit financing still heavily depended on capital inflows through foreign purchases of debt securities. Moreover, a substantial share of these purchases has been finding its way into the rapidly rising official reserves of foreign central banks, notably those of emerging East Asian economies.

As a result of persistent current account deficits, the US net international investment position has continued to deteriorate, reaching an estimated $3.3 trillion or 27 percent of GDP – barring any valuation change (Figure 7.3). However, its pace of deterioration has not been in line with the continuation of large current account deficits over recent years because dollar depreciation has boosted the dollar value of US external assets abroad.

Japan

Japan has been running the largest current account surplus over most of the last 15 years, reaching $164 billion in 2005, or 3.4 percent of GDP. While the largest in the world, the size of its surplus is only 20 percent of the US deficit. Japan's current account surplus has been financed largely by net private capital outflows and the central bank's foreign exchange reserve accumulation,

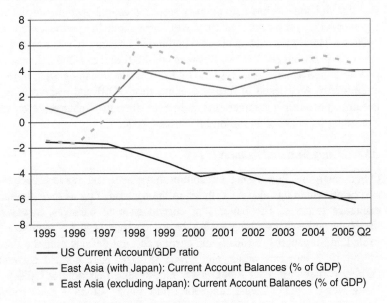

Figure 7.3 US and East Asia: current account balance (% of GDP).
Source: Datastream and world development indicators.

the latter being particularly conspicuous in 2003–2004 when the country saw private net capital inflows. The consequence of persistent current account surpluses is a trend increase in the country's net international investment position, reaching an estimated $1.9 trillion, or 45 percent of GDP, in 2005.

Japan's foreign exchange reserves also rose fast over the recent years and stood at $834 billion at end-2005. The Bank of Japan accumulated reserve assets until 2004 as a result of the authorities' desire to avoid rapid yen appreciation in the face of persistent price deflation and uncertain and fragile economic conditions following the 'lost decade' of economic stagnation. The authorities' view was that sudden yen appreciation could derail the country's incipient economic recovery and put further downward pressure on price levels. However, currency market interventions ended in mid-March 2004, and the reserves have hardly risen since then due to the absence of official purchases of reserve assets.

PRC

With an estimated $150 billion in current account surplus, PRC was the world's second largest surplus country in 2005. As in the case of Japan, PRC has been running current account surpluses throughout the 1990s and the early 2000s, except in 1993, and the size of the surplus began to rise visibly from 2002, reaching 7.9 percent of GDP in 2005. Noteworthy is the fact that the country has continuously recorded capital account surpluses, together with current account surpluses, throughout the period except in 1992 and 1998. This led to a massive buildup of foreign exchange reserves, particularly during 2003–2005. Between end-2002 and end-2005, the country's foreign exchange reserves rose by $530 billion, reaching $822 billion at end-2005. As a result of further accumulation of official reserves, PRC became the world's number one holder of foreign exchange reserves, exceeding Japan, at $854 billion in February 2006.

ASEAN members and Asian NIEs

Other emerging East Asian economies have also run current account surpluses, which has also contributed to the accumulation of their foreign exchange reserves. The patterns of current account balances, however, have been somewhat different across these economies. ASEAN members – excluding Singapore – basically ran current account deficits until the time of the 1997 currency crisis, and began to experience current account surpluses afterward. Four Asian newly industrialized economies (NIEs) – Hong Kong, China; Korea; Singapore; and Taipei, China – ran current account surpluses throughout the period, except that Korea had experienced deficits until 1997 and began recording surpluses afterward. Data for former crisis-affected countries – Korea, Indonesia, Malaysia, the Philippines, and Thailand – exhibited a massive swing in their aggregate current account before and after the financial crisis, i.e., from a deficit of $54 billion in 1996 to a surplus of $70 billion in 1998.

In addition to PRC, many emerging market economies in East Asia began to accumulate foreign reserve assets. The value of global foreign exchange reserves – held primarily by central banks – rose by more than $2.2 trillion from roughly $2.0 trillion in 2000 to $4.2 trillion in 2005. Four East Asian economies – PRC; Japan; Taipei,China; and Korea – accounted for more than 60 percent of this global reserve increase.

Oil exporting countries

Rising crude oil prices caused many oil exporting countries to run large current account surpluses. Five major oil exporting countries – Kuwait, Libya, Nigeria, Saudi Arabia, and Venezuela – began to register sizable current account surpluses in 2000, totaling $171 billion in 2005. Among them, Saudi Arabia has been the largest surplus country. Russia also bene-fited enormously from oil price hikes, recording $84 billion in 2005. The combined surplus of these oil exporting countries and Russia was roughly comparable to that of emerging East Asia at $255 billion each.

Factors behind the global imbalances: savings and investment imbalances

Recent growth in US current account deficits, and the corresponding surpluses in other economies, has sparked debate about the causes of these imbalances. A variety of factors can explain these recent trends. Bernanke (2005) argues that a 'global saving glut' explains the growth of US current account deficits – as well as the relatively low level of global long-term interest rates – while Rajan (2006) argues that 'inadequate investment' in other parts of the world is the primary cause. The most fundamental factor is the pattern of domestic savings and investment in the United States and in other economies. Global payments imbalances should be analyzed from a global perspective as they are a joint outcome of the savings-investment relationships of major economies in the world. However, the sheer size of the US deficits suggests that the primary cause should be found in the United States, while additional factors may be sought in East Asia and recent hikes in crude oil prices.

United States

The large buildup of US current account deficits essentially reflects a worsening savings and investment balance in the United States. As Figure 7.4

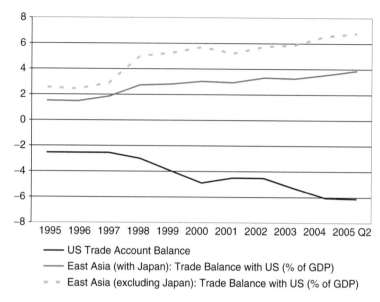

Figure 7.4 US trade account balance and East Asia trade account balance with US (% of GDP).
Source: Datastream and world development indicators.

indicates, the United States has had a relatively stable gross fixed investment rate at around 19 percent of GDP throughout the last 25 years. However, its gross domestic savings rate has been declining as a trend from around 20 percent of GDP in the early 1980s to around 14 percent in recent years. This decline has been particularly noteworthy since 1997 when the gross savings rate was 18 percent. With a domestic gross investment rate at 20 percent of GDP, a low and declining US gross savings rate – the lowest among the advanced economies – has resulted in US current account deficits.

US net domestic savings have declined secularly over time (Figure 7.5). Disaggregating net savings into three parts – personal, corporate, and public savings – one finds that personal savings have been declining as a trend and public savings have declined since 2000. Net corporate savings have been steady at about 2.5 percent of GDP and have recently gone up to 3.5 percent in 2005 due to rapidly improving corporate profits.[2] Personal savings have declined from 3.4 percent of GDP in 1995 to 1.7 percent in 2000, and to a historically unprecedented negative 0.3 percent of GDP in 2005. This decline in personal savings rate reflects a rise in personal consumption due to the

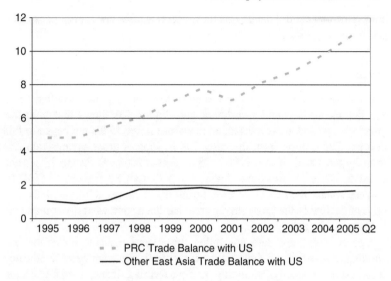

Figure 7.5 PRC trade balance with US, and other East Asian countries trade balance with US (% of GDP).
Source: Datastream and world development indicators.

impact of housing price boom and ensuing capital gains on household consumption spending. Net public sector savings declined from 2.4 percent of GDP in 2000 to negative 2.6 percent in 2005 after bouncing back from the trough of negative 3.7 percent or GDP recorded in 2003.

The observed close correlation between total net savings and net government savings indicates that the country's overall net savings are strongly affected by the cyclical movements of government net savings. A large decline in the net government savings rate between 2000 and 2003 in the order of 6 percent of GDP was an important factor that reduced total net domestic savings, and a continuous decline in net personal savings between 2003 and 2005 in the order of 2 percent of GDP also contributed to further declines in US net savings.

The large size of US financial markets and the global role of the US dollar as the most dominant international currency may have also contributed to the persistence of US current account deficits, by encouraging global investors to hold dollar-denominated assets and, hence, allowing the United States to continue to spend more than it earns. Large and efficient financial markets in the United States are clearly beneficial to many foreign investors trying to diversify their portfolios – including multinational firms, fund managers, and central banks   as these markets offer low transactions costs and liquidity risks.

Japan

The recent expansion of Japan's current account surpluses resulted from a widening savings and investment gap. Figure 7.6 shows that both the gross savings and gross investment rates rose in the 1980s but began to fall in a parallel fashion from the early 1990s. Japan's gross savings rate fell from 34 percent of GDP in 1990 to 28 percent in 2000 and then to 25 percent in 2005, while its gross investment rate fell from 33 percent of GDP to 26 percent and then to 23 percent during the same period. Essentially, the pace of decline in the gross savings rate has been somewhat faster than that in the gross investment rate.

Japan's investment rate has fallen for several reasons. Following the bursting of asset price bubbles in the early 1990s, the country suffered from large excess capacity, mounting non-performing loans, banking sector difficulties, and economic stagnation, which made Japanese firms more

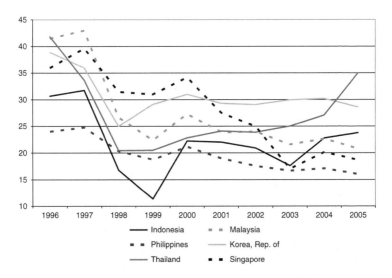

Figure 7.6 Gross domestic investment/GDP at current prices* (%).
Source: ARIC indicators.

Note: For Singapore, data used are in constant prices.

cautious about undertaking new domestic investment. Japan's real GDP growth rate was a mere 1.1 percent per annum during the long period of economic stagnation (1991–2002), and it was even lower at an average 0.1 percent in more recent years (1998–2002). Price deflation also weakened private investment.

Between 1995 and 2005, Japan's corporate sector went from being a net borrower of funds of 2 to 3 percent of GDP to a net lender of funds equivalent to nearly 15 percent of GDP. During the same period, net savings in Japan's household sector fell from 10 percent to about 3 percent of GDP while its public sector became a large net borrower of funds. Essentially rising net corporate savings more than offset the declining net household savings and the net public sector borrowing, which explains much of the recent expansion of Japan's current account surpluses.

PRC

The large current account surpluses of PRC have resulted primarily from a high savings rate, whose pace of increase has been faster than that of investment rates. In contrast to Japan, PRC has seen rising investment and savings as a trend over the last 25 years. PRC's gross domestic investment rate rose from an average 35 percent of GDP in the 1980s to 38 percent in the 1990s and then to a projected 46 percent of GDP in 2005 (prior to its GDP revision), which is very high. Its gross domestic savings rate rose even more rapidly from 35 percent of GDP in the 1980s to 41 percent in the 1990s and then a projected 50 percent in 2005, which is the highest in the world.

Several factors contribute to PRC's high savings rate in both the household and corporate sectors. The country's 'one child' policy, enacted to control its population growth, has contributed to households' rising savings rates by increasing the share of older groups within its labor forces, as older workers typically earn and save more than younger workers. The absence of a strong social safety net – including adequate public pensions and health care – has increased the need for precautionary and retirement household savings. The absence of well-developed financial markets and consumer credit mechanisms may have also contributed to high savings as many people are compelled to save large amounts of cash before making purchases rather than by taking consumer loans. In addition, deficient financial markets may have induced local businesses to pile up retained earnings. Essentially, the ageing of PRC's workforce, absence of an adequate social safety net, and the limited access of households to credit are the major factors behind PRC's high and rising savings rate.[3]

PRC's foreign exchange reserves have increased rapidly due to its rising current account surpluses, net private capital inflows, and inflows through errors and omissions under its tightly managed exchange rate system. The motivations for accumulating large foreign exchange reserves are somewhat different between Japan and PRC. In Japan, reserves were accumulated as a result of the authorities' attempt to ensure sustained economic recovery from the decade-long stagnation and to end persistent price deflation that plagued its economy. In PRC, reserve accumulation took place mainly from a desire to maintain stable exchange rates in the process of economic development, reform, and transition. The Chinese policymakers regarded rate stability as essential for internal monetary stability needed for sustained economic growth, outward-oriented industrialization, and employment expansion. The policy of maintaining tightly managed exchange rates vis-à-vis the US dollar and of accumulating US dollar reserves has prompted some authors to call it the emergence of a 'revived Bretton Woods system' (Dooley, *et al.*, 2005). With a *de facto* dollar-pegged arrangement, PRC has been able to sustain current account surpluses and supporting buoyant FDI inflows and strong export-led growth.

NIEs and ASEAN members

Current account surpluses of other emerging market economies reflect a shortfall of their domestic investment relative to domestic savings. Situations are different, however, between those economies that were directly affected by the 1997–1998 financial crisis and those not directly affected. Economies that were not directly affected – such as Singapore; Hong Kong,China; and Taipei,China – have maintained high savings and investment rates with savings exceeding investment. Their gross domestic investment rates began to decline and the gross savings rates began to rise in the 2000s, which contributed to larger current account surpluses.

Former crisis-affected economies – Korea and the four middle-income ASEAN countries including Indonesia, Malaysia, the Philippines, and Thailand – had maintained high investment exceeding savings, prior to the crisis. For example, middle-income ASEAN's gross domestic investment rate was an average 34 percent of GDP during 1990–1997, while its average gross domestic savings rate was 32 percent. Korea had a gross investment rate of 37 percent of GDP and a gross savings rate of 36 percent during the same period. As a result, these economies had current account deficits. However, they saw a collapse of investment activities in the aftermath of the crisis; middle-income ASEAN experienced a fall of investment rates from 33 to 20 percent of GDP between 1997 and 1998 and Korea from 36 to 25 percent between these two years, thereby suddenly running current account surpluses. Their investment rates have not recovered yet while the savings rates remained roughly unchanged. These sharp reductions in investment contributed to lower growth as well as persistent current account surpluses among these countries.

They have rapidly accumulated foreign exchange reserves. For example, the four Asian NIEs increased reserves from $390 billion in 2000 to $700 billion in 2005, while middle-income ASEAN from $100 billion to $172 billion during the same period. They did so for reasons different from Japan or PRC. They accumulated reserves from a desire to build up a 'war chest' against severe external shocks, sudden changes in capital flows, or speculative attacks on their currencies after having gone through the painful experience of the Asian financial crisis.

Oil exporting countries and Russia

Oil exporting countries and Russia have been running large current account surpluses due to rising domestic savings. Their gross domestic investment rate has been steady at about 20 percent of GDP over the last ten years, while the gross domestic savings rate has risen from 27 percent to 35 percent of GDP. Large and increasing oil revenues led to the emergence of large and rising savings.

Issues and problems of the imbalances

Perception of 'sustainability'

The present current account imbalances can be sustained as long as international investors are willing to finance the US current account deficits on favorable terms. A country may be able to run current account deficits indefinitely provided capital inflows promote domestic investment, productivity, and economic growth. On this ground some have argued that the current global imbalances are sustainable at least for the foreseeable future.

This point must be discussed in the context of net external debt sustainability. As long as the net international investment position (NIIP) relative to GDP is maintained at a reasonable level the country's payment of investment income will be limited and international investors will continue to have confidence in the economy. However, if the NIIP/GDP ratio declines to a very low level, such confidence may not be sustained. Although US current account deficits have raised the level of its net external liabilities from 16 percent of GDP in 2000 to an estimated 27 percent in 2005, the United States continued to earn net investment income until 2004 and has begun to pay only a small amount of net investment income abroad in 2005. For example it earned $30 billion in net investment income in 2004 despite a stock of NIIP of negative $2.5 trillion, and paid only $5 billion in net investment income against an NIIP of negative $3.3 trillion in 2005.

This relationship between the net international investment position and net investment income reflects that rates of return on US assets are much higher than those on US liabilities to foreigners. As long as US investors earn significantly higher rates of return abroad than foreign investors do in the United States, the impact of accumulating a negative NIIP on net investment income is limited. If past experience is of any guide, a further reduction of NIIP in the order of 20 percent of GDP may increase payment of net investment income by only 0.5 percent of GDP. Hence the United States still has large room for continuing to run current account deficits. Furthermore, with gradual depreciation of the US dollar, a large current account deficit will not lead to a rapid accumulation of net external liabilities.

Eichengreen (2006) examines three arguments for the 'sustainability' of the US net external liability, i.e., the new economy, the dark matter, and the savvy investor. The 'new economy' theory emphasizes that the high productivity growth and high rates of return in the United States have induced and will induce foreign investors to invest in US assets; the 'dark matter' story argues that the existing balance of payments statistics do not accurately measure the true wealth of US firms with value creating assets abroad and that, if such hidden wealth were fully captured, US current account deficits would not be growing; and the 'savvy investor' view says that sophisticated US investors can earn high rates of return abroad while foreign investors earn low rates of return, often incurring capital losses due to dollar depreciation, by holding US assets.

Eichengreen convincingly demonstrates that these three arguments are not mutually consistent with each other and that the current trend of global payments imbalances cannot continue indefinitely as no country can experience ever-rising net external liabilities, relative to GDP, without bound. In the long run, the deterioration of NIIP will create huge burdens in the current account through ever-rising payments of net investment income to foreigners. This would eventually convince international investors that the country will not be able to continue to make such net income payments without substantially changing economic policies or market environments. Or, as the deficit widens, there may be a political concern about the deficit – thereby generating protectionist sentiments – or about rising capital inflows and growing net external liabilities – thereby generating nationalistic backlash toward foreigners buying into the United States.

Possible consequences

Consensus exists among economists that current trends cannot continue indefinitely and the existing global imbalances will stop widening and start unwinding at some time in the future (see Bernanke 2005; Blanchard, Giavazzi and Sa 2005; Edwards 2005; Eichengreen 2006; Obstfeld and Rogoff 2004, 2005; Rajan 2006; Summers 2006). Adjustment may take two forms: orderly adjustment through increases in US savings and/or increases in spending in surplus countries; or disorderly adjustment involving sharp declines in the US dollar, sharp increases in US interest rates, and sharp declines in US asset prices. The latter scenario may lead to a severe recession in the US and world economy.

It is, therefore, important to bring down US current account deficits. Recent estimates suggest that to bring about a one percentage point reduction in the ratio of US current account deficit to GDP, the dollar would have to depreciate by anywhere from 8 to 18 percent—depending on the various parameter values.[4] This implies that to reduce the US current account deficit to about 2.5 percent, the dollar will have to depreciate by anywhere from 32 to 72 percent. The longer the delay in bringing about the adjustment, the higher would be the eventual dollar depreciation, and the more chaotic the adjustment process. If an orderly resolution of current global imbalances is not achieved through appropriate policy actions by the major countries involved, the world economy runs the risk of a chaotic adjustment: a crisis of confidence in the US economy, rapid unloading of the large stock of US dollar assets held by international investors, a sudden and sharp US dollar depreciation along with skyrocketing US interest rates and collapsing asset prices, and even perhaps unprecedented protectionist measures by the United States. The end result of such a disorderly adjustment could be a deep and prolonged global recession.

A sudden and steep depreciation of the dollar, together with a sharp hike in long-term interest rates, would substantially dampen the already modest expansion projected for Japan, the euro-area, and many emerging market economies in East Asia. Dollar depreciation will certainly reduce these economies' international price competitiveness and create large capital losses on US dollar assets – such as foreign exchange reserves. On the other hand, it can have some positive effects on certain economies with large dollar-denominated external debt as it reduces the real net external debt burden; but such positive effects could easily be more than offset if dollar depreciation leads to a hard landing of the US economy.

A shared approach to resolving the global imbalances

The unpleasant consequences of a dollar hard-landing scenario prompt a search for policies that could bring about a smooth transition to a more sustainable level of global imbalances. A shared approach is needed to address the essential aspects of global payments imbalances and to avoid a shared dollar crash.

Stimulating national savings in the United States

First, the United States should make the foremost effort to increase national – both private and government – savings. Sections of the US tax code that discourage savings should clearly be reformed as appropriate. A more aggressive pension program may be put in place to stimulate personal savings for retirement, above and beyond the existing social security system. This is even more important as health care, social security, and other entitlement programs must also be reformed given their large projected impact on future public spending and hence fiscal balance. This expenditure reduction will have to be accompanied by expenditure switching through real dollar depreciation. That is, the United States must increase the output of tradable goods and reduce the output of non-tradable goods and services, while at the same time substantially containing the spending on all types of goods and services.

Obviously fiscal consolidation of the United States is crucial, not least because it is desirable in its own right. However, given that both Japan and the euro-area also need fiscal consolidation – both facing higher public debt and greater ageing-related fiscal pressures than in the United States (see Figure 7.7) – the US effort at fiscal consolidation may have limited contribution to global current account rebalancing. Nonetheless, as fiscal adjustment can have immediate impacts on current accounts, a quick fiscal policy action on the part of the United States is highly desirable.

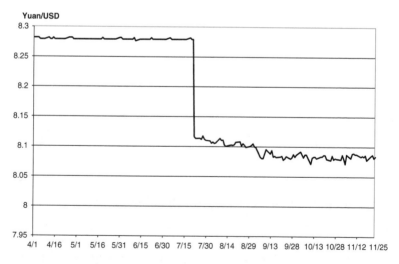

Figure 7.7 Actual Yuan exchange rate against US doller (Daily Figures).

Structural reforms in Japan and the euro-area

Second, Japan and the euro-area need to pursue structural reforms to ensure sustained economic growth and further improvement of growth performance. Japan should continue to pursue reforms to eliminate regulatory impediments to private sector economic activities and to enhance total factor productivity as its workforces are shrinking and ageing and capital-labor ratios are already high. The euro-area should focus on reforms to make the labor market more flexible and to improve competitiveness. Essentially, structural reforms to strengthen incentives for labor supply, corporate investment, and household consumption are critical. Japan's strong economic recovery in recent years is a bright sign in this direction as it is expected to further expand both investment and consumption.[5]

Greater exchange rate flexibility in PRC

Third, PRC should stimulate domestic demand, particularly consumption as its investment rate is already at a historically high level. Given that the rates of return on new investment are declining, that the rapid investment growth can be a source of economic overheating, and that a large part of investment is financed by state-owned commercial banks, it is very important for the country to rein in investment and to focus on 'quality' investment with high social rates of return, such as for environmental protection and energy efficiency. Measures to stimulate consumption include: reforms of financial systems to help expand consumer credit; establishment of social sector protection so as to reduce the need for high levels of precautionary savings; and greater exchange rate flexibility thereby allowing currency appreciation so as to reduce the rapid pace of reserve accumulation, raise real income, and rebalance growth patterns.

In order to contain the rapid accumulation of foreign exchange reserves, the authorities are advised to implement greater exchange rate flexibility and further liberalization of capital outflow control. Rapid accumulation of reserves can eventually have serious monetary consequences domestically, as sterilization policies cannot be maintained for a long time. Growing domestic liquidity can feed into further overheating of the economy. By allowing greater exchange rate flexibility the authorities can slow down the pace of reserve accumulation and retain a higher degree of monetary policy autonomy – such as adopting high interest rate policy to combat overheating. In addition, liberalization of autonomous capital outflows can ease the upward pressure on the yuan and, hence, the need to purchase reserve assets through currency market intervention.

What PRC does with regard to its exchange rate regime is also crucial for the region's exchange rate regime. The revaluation of the yuan against the dollar by 2.1 percent and the shift from a *de facto* US dollar peg to a managed floating regime with reference to a basket of currencies on 21 July 2005 was a welcome initial step in imparting greater flexibility to PRC's exchange rate policy. However, the rate has not fluctuated much since the policy shift, and the yuan–dollar rate has moved up by only about 3.5 percent altogether. Although the new system is supposed to be managed with reference to a basket of currencies, in practice, it has maintained a *de facto* dollar-pegged regime, or a basket currency regime with a very high weight on the dollar. Building on the July 2005 policy shift, PRC, therefore, needs to move to greater flexibility in its exchange rate regime.

Reviving private investment in former crisis-affected East Asian economies

Fourth, for other emerging East Asian economies, particularly those affected by the 1997–1998 financial crisis, stimulating investment is of most importance for not only reducing current account surpluses but also sustaining growth. Investment to GDP ratios in Indonesia, Malaysia, the Philippines, and Thailand have not risen much from the lows reached in the aftermath of the financial crisis. Of course, since one of the causes of the crisis was the large buildup of fixed assets in the pre-crisis years – the so-called investment bubble – investment rates are not expected to quickly recover to pre-crisis levels. However, a significant increase in investment rates from the current levels would be both desirable and necessary for sustaining economic growth in the ASEAN region, because there are still large unexploited investment opportunities with high social and/or private rates of returns. There is, therefore, a need to improve the investment climate in these countries.

Improving investment climate requires efforts on many fronts, but perhaps most crucial is to establish market friendly environments for both domestic and foreign firms. Many ASEAN countries have made significant progress in eliminating regulatory impediments to domestic and foreign businesses and in strengthening industrial infrastructure and legal frameworks to promote private investment. First, many governments have made efforts to improve and upgrade their industrial and social infrastructure – railways, roads, ports, power, information, and communication, etc. – for private sector activities. However, more needs to be done in this area. Second, governments have strengthened legal and regulatory frameworks concerning investment by domestic and foreign firms so as to address the cumbersome procedures for, and the high costs of, undertaking businesses. They have been introducing the 'rule of law', a key foundation of any market economy – including protection of private ownership (and intellectual property rights), enforcement of contracts (such as claims and debts), and regulatory transparency and predictability. However, many governments have yet to effectively implement these measures. Third, governments have made efforts to make labor management and employment practices flexible to encourage domestic business activities by private firms – whether foreign or local SMEs.

Stimulating domestic investment in oil exporting countries

Finally, oil exporting countries could increase their domestic investment. Some of this spending may be used to expand oil sector production – including refineries – to enhance the future productive capacity and help ensure adequate future supplies of oil for the global economy. Another type of spending could be made for the purpose of strengthening the countries' industrial and social infrastructure to encourage domestic economic activities and improve citizens' quality of life.

Implications for East Asia's monetary and financial cooperation

Economic surveillance and financial safeguards

For emerging economies in East Asia, the most urgent priority is to continue taking advantage of current favorable external environments while pursuing the domestic macroeconomic and structural reforms necessary for long-term economic growth and stability. This strategy involves building on recent macroeconomic gains – larger foreign exchange reserves, lower short-term external debt, greater exchange rate flexibility, low inflation, sound fiscal conditions, and steady growth – to address structural weaknesses in their financial systems and external asset-liability management.

Those East Asian economies that have accumulated more foreign exchange reserves than is necessary to meet prudential demand for liquidity and protection against volatile capital flows may need to reconsider the policy, because continuing reserve accumulation far in excess of these needs carries its own costs and risks. First, accumulation of a large scale of reserves will eventually have serious domestic monetary consequences as the effectiveness of sterilization diminishes over time. Second, the quasi-fiscal costs associated with sterilization operations will rise over time. Third, the risk of capital losses on reserves will mount as the risk of dollar depreciation becomes large. Hence there is a need for greater exchange rate flexibility.

In this context, the East Asian economies need to strengthen their regional economic surveillance and liquidity provision mechanism, the Chiang Mai Initiative (CMI). Regional economic surveillance should focus more on exchange rate issues – in addition to the monitoring of regional and country economic conditions, financial developments and short-term capital flows – so as to facilitate smooth international adjustment, to reduce risks due to excessive accumulation of reserve assets, and to avoid large misalignments of exchange rates at the regional level. Finance ministers and central bank Governors in the region need to establish a framework for their mutual policy dialogue. As many economies in the region are increasingly integrated financially and may face volatile capital flows with the rising the risk of disorderly exchange rate adjustment, they must strengthen the CMI as a financial-safeguard, reserve-pooling arrangement. This would entail enlarging currency swap lines and credits, multilateralizing swap arrangements, and further loosening the linkage with IMF conditionality. All of these must also be accompanied by enhanced surveillance – for example, through the creation of a professional, independent secretariat capable of formulating adjustment policies in the event of a liquidity crisis.

Asian bond market development

One of the reasons for the large pool of Asia's savings not adequately being invested in Asia is the lack of efficient financial intermediation in the region. Despite the presence of massive investment opportunities in Asia, the excess savings simply find their way to the global capital markets. Paradoxically, a portion of this surplus is also recycled back to be used for investment in Asia. Several East Asian economies were severely damaged by the 1997–1998 financial crisis due to the excessive reliance on domestic bank financing and short-term foreign currency financing which was highly volatile – the well-known 'double mismatch' problem. Being insufficiently supervised and governed, many East Asian banks were paralyzed by the crisis and, as a result, were unable to perform ordinary financial intermediation functions. Alternative financing sources, such as local currency bond markets, have been considered necessary to mobilize Asian savings for Asian investment. Development of local currency bond markets can also make the Asian financial system more balanced with a healthier banking system and a deeper bond market as two wheels of the system.

Development of local currency bond markets can allow financial intermediaries and savers to find the right investment opportunities in the region by reducing information asymmetry which is an inherent problem in any financial system. Measures to develop local currency bond markets in the region have proceeded at two levels – national and regional. At the national level, building the supporting infrastructure required for a well-functioning bond market has been considered crucial, as are the development of a legal and regulatory framework based on international best practices and the nurturing of a high quality domestic credit rating industry. At the regional level, measures have been addressed to facilitate cross-border flow of surplus funds through the bond market, so that countries with surplus savings could channel these savings into countries with large investment needs.

Recent national and regional initiatives to develop bond markets, including the Asian Bond Market Initiative (ABMI) by ASEAN+3 Finance ministers and the Asian Bond Fund (ABF) initiative by the Executive Meeting of East Asia-Pacific Central Banks (EMEAP), are laudable. Partly because of these initiatives at both the national and regional levels, the size of local currency bond markets in emerging East Asia more than quadrupled between 1997 and 2005, reaching $1.7 trillion in 2005. Building on these initiatives, continued efforts are required to develop deep and liquid local currency bond markets.

Collective appreciation of regional exchange rates

East Asia needs to work jointly to achieve a desired adjustment of the exchange rate as part of the global effort at orderly adjustment of global imbalances. This requires exchange rate policy coordination among the East Asian economies – collective appreciation of the exchange rates vis-à-vis the US dollar, while keeping the intra-regional exchange rates stable. Maintaining relative stability of intra-regional exchange rates is desirable as the adjustment costs will be spread across a large number of East Asian economies and will be minimized from the perspective of individual economies subject, of course, to the US policy correction. For this purpose, it is essential that the yuan becomes more flexible vis-à-vis the US dollar so that the East Asian currencies can appreciate collectively.

If no global effort is pursued among the major industrialized countries and the US current account deficit persists, the risk of abrupt and sharp adjustment of the dollar will mount. If such dollar adjustment becomes unavoidable in a crisis or a crisis-like scenario, it is still desirable for all East Asian economies to let their currencies appreciate together against the dollar in a coordinated fashion. By agreeing region-wide on such exchange rate policy coordination in advance, economies in East Asia can have a mechanism to manage this potentially difficult process without much confusion. For this purpose, the policy dialogue mechanism among the region's Finance ministers and central bank Governors can play a key role. The PRC authorities need to allow the yuan to exhibit greater flexibility so that it could move together with the other East Asian currencies at a time of sharp US dollar adjustment.

With or without a global effort at orderly resolution of global imbalances, PRC needs to adopt greater flexibility in its exchange rate regime, which would foster greater exchange rate flexibility in East Asia as a whole and provide greater opportunity for collective exchange rate action. This would also slow down the pace of foreign exchange reserve accumulation in East Asia and thus end the 'revived Bretton Woods system'. More importantly it can signify the beginning of the formation of an East Asian currency zone where exchange rates fluctuate vis-à-vis the US dollar but are kept relatively stable intra-regionally.

Conclusion

The paper has argued that the current pace of growing US current account deficits is not sustainable in the long run. If it persists over time, the risk of a dollar hard landing and US and global economic recession rises. Reducing them to a manageable level in an orderly way will require globally concerted efforts to implement necessary macroeconomic and structural policy measures among the major economies – the United States, Japan, euro-area, PRC, other emerging East Asian economies, and oil exporting countries – as well as an orderly, market-based change in real exchange rates to facilitate international payments adjustment.

A global strategy that attempts to secure a sufficient reduction of global payments imbalances consists of the following measures: first, the United States needs to boost national savings, particularly household savings – while fiscal consolidation is necessary in both the United States and in Japan and the euro-area – in order to restore a fundamental savings-investment balance. Second, Japan and the euro-area need to pursue structural reforms to ensure sustained economic growth and domestic demand expansion. Third, PRC and other emerging East Asian economies must stimulate consumption (particularly in PRC) and/or investment (particularly in ASEAN), together with greater exchange rate flexibility. Fourth, oil exporting countries need to increase their domestic investment, particularly for expanding oil sector production.

US dollar depreciation would help reduce US current account deficits through its positive impact on the trade balance and its stabilizing influence on the net external liability position. It is only through a combination of aggregate demand, structural and exchange rate instruments that the necessary rebalancing of global demand can be achieved in a non-disruptive manner. For emerging market economies in East Asia, there is scope for using greater exchange rate flexibility for rebalancing the sources of growth away from exports to domestic demand. It is encouraging that PRC has made the initial move in imparting greater flexibility to its exchange rate regime by ending the yuan peg to the dollar and moving to a managed float with reference to a basket of currencies. Malaysia also followed suit with a similar shift in its exchange rate regime. Building on this policy shift, PRC and Malaysia need to increase flexibility of their currencies against the dollar.

In addition, the East Asian economies could be most severely affected by abrupt and sharp exchange rate changes in the event of a sudden crash of the US dollar and, hence, need to be prepared for regional exchange rate policy coordination. They are advised to allow their currencies to appreciate collectively, while maintaining intra-regional exchange rate stability, so that the costs of adjustment can be spread among them. This will lead to the creation of a natural currency zone, which exhibits rate flexibility vis-à-vis the US dollar and rate stability vis-à-vis other currencies in the region, in a way to support the region's close economic linkages formed over the last several decades.

Notes

1 21 April 2006, The author is grateful to Marc Uzan for inviting him to contribute this paper to the Journal and to Wilhelmina Paz and Richard Supangan for their efficient research assistance. The findings, interpretations, and conclusions expressed in the paper are entirely those of the author alone and do not necessarily represent the view of the Asian Development Bank, its executive directors, or the countries they represent.
2 The US corporate sector actually has a savings-investment surplus. The surplus in the corporate sector is not an exclusive feature of the United States; it reflects the ongoing corporate balance sheet restoration in the wake of the world-wide stock market correction in 2000–2001, with rapidly growing profits unable to catch up with investment.
3 See *OECD Economic Survey of China*, Paris, 2005.
4 Blanchard, Giavazzi, and Sa (2005), Obstfeld and Rogoff (2004, 2005), and Chinn (2005).
5 Park (2006) emphasizes the critical role of Japan's expanding aggregate demand in the orderly resolution of global imbalances.

Bibliography

Bernanke, Ben. (2005) 'The Global Savings Glut and the US Current Account Deficit'. Remarks at the Sandridge Lecture (10 March), Virginia Association of Economics, Richmond.
Blanchard, Oliver, Francesco Giavazzi, and Filipa Sa. (2005) 'The US Current Account and the Dollar'. *Brookings Papers on Economic Activity*, 1, pp. 1–65.
Chinn, Menzie. (2005) 'Doomed to Deficits? Aggregate US Trade Flows Re-Examined'. NBER Working Paper No. 9521 (April), National Bureau of Economic Research.
Dooley, Michael, David Folkerts-Landau, and Peter Garber. (2005) *International Financial Stability: Asia Interest Rates and the Dollar*, Deutsche Bank (27 October).

Edwards, Sebastian. (2005) 'Is the US Current Account Deficit Sustainable? If Not, How Costly Is Adjustment Likely to Be?' *Brookings Papers on Economic Activity*, 1, pp. 211–288.

Eichengreen, Barry. (2006) 'Global Imbalances: The New Economy, the Dark Matter, the Savvy Investor, and the Standard Analysis'. Mimeographed (March 2006), University of California, Berkeley. [Forthcoming in the *Journal of Policy Modeling*.]

Obstfeld, Maurice and Kenneth Rogoff. (2004) 'The Unsustainable US Current Account Position Revisited'. NBER Working Paper No. 10869 (October), National Bureau of Economic Research.

Obstfeld, Maurice and Kenneth Rogoff. (2005) 'Global Current Account Imbalances and Exchange Rate Adjustments'. *Brookings Papers on Economic Activity*, 1, pp. 67–146.

Park, Yung Chul. (2006) 'Global Imbalances and East Asia's Policy Adjustments'. Mimeographed (January 2006), Seoul National University, Seoul.

Rajan, Raghuram. (2006) 'Perspectives on Global Imbalances'. www.imf.org (23 January 2006).

Roubini, Nouriel and Brad Setser. (2005) 'Will the Bretton Woods 2 Regime Unravel Soon? The Risk of a Hard Landing in 2005–2006'. A paper presented to the symposium of the Federal Reserve Bank of San Francisco and the University of California, Berkeley, 'Revised Bretton Woods System: A New Paradigm for Asian Development?' (February 2005), San Francisco.

Summers, Lawrence. (2006) 'Reflections on Global Account Imbalances and Emerging Markets Reserve Accumulation'. Mimeographed (24 March 2006), Harvard University, Cambridge. www.president.harvard.edu/speeches.

Yoshitomi, Masaru. (2006) 'Global Imbalances and East Asian Monetary Cooperation'. Duck-Koo Chung and Barry Eichengreen, (eds.), *Toward an East Asian Exchange Rate Regime*, (forthcoming, 2006).

8 Asia is learning the wrong lessons from its 1997–98 financial crisis

The rising risks of a new and different type of financial crisis in Asia

Nouriel Roubini

This year – 2007 – is the tenth anniversary of the Asian financial crisis that started in 1997 with the spring pressures and eventually July collapse of the Thai baht. The crisis soon spread to Indonesia, Malaysia and by October 1997 hit South Korea. All but Malaysia were forced to rely on painful IMF austerity programs to control the liquidity runs that accelerated the financial severity of the crisis. While other countries in the region did not experience as severe a crisis as in the four economies above significant currency and financial pressures also hit Hong Kong, Taiwan, Singapore, China and the Philippines leading to a sharp economic slowdown even in the countries not directly enveloped in a significant crisis. This is why the crisis of 1997–1998 is referred to as the Asian Financial Crisis.

While market and economies were in free fall in 1997–1998 (with severe economic recession in the crisis countries in 1998) the economic and financial outlook looks very different today: the economies in the region are booming with growth last year averaging 8 percent and financial markets are bubbly with rising currencies, rising stock markets and record low sovereign spread. What a difference relative to the crisis mood of 1997–1998.

Is it all rosy and safe in Asia or are there new financial risks and vulnerabilities? The region is currently exuberant about its economic recovery after the crisis and its current economic and financial buoyancy, as the current celebrations at the fortieth anniversary of the Asian Development Bank attest; but there are reasons to worry about the future as Asia seems to have understood well some of the lessons of the 1997–1998 crisis while at the same time having also learned some of the wrong lessons from that crisis. Indeed, the currency and financial policies in Asia today are risking planting the seeds of a new and different financial crisis in the region in the medium term.

On the surface financial and economic conditions in Asia are excellent and look the opposite of those in 1997–1998, but below the surface some trouble is brewing and significant financial imbalances are building up. Let us consider first the apparent differences between today and 1997 and consider next the new financial vulnerabilities of the region. Let's consider five factors that, at least on the surface, look very different today relative to 1997.

First, in 1997 most of the countries in the region – especially those that experience a crisis – were running large current account deficits, they had regimes of semi-fixed exchange rates, their currencies were overvalued and they were experiencing negative terms of trade shocks (such as the fall in semi-conductor prices in 1996 that worsened the Korean trade deficit). Fixed rates led to overvalued currencies (as the Asian followed the US dollar in its upward trend since mid-1995) and overvalued currencies led to loss of competitiveness and rising current account deficits that eventually became unsustainable. Once the financial vulnerabilities of the region emerged because of global shocks (worsening terms of trade, stronger US dollar, concerns about a global slowdown) the sudden stop of capital inflows led to currency crises and a sudden lack of financing of those large current account deficits. The crises ensued. Today, on the surface the conditions look just like the opposite: most of the countries in the region run current account surpluses, they have abandoned fixed exchange rates and have moved to floats or managed floats, their currencies are somewhat undervalued, certainly not overvalued and terms of trade have been improving (high commodity prices for commodity exporters and high prices for the intermediate and final goods produced by the manufacturing exporters).

Second, in 1997 there were severe balance sheet vulnerabilities that eventually triggered the crisis: maturity mismatches leading to rollover/liquidity risk; currency mismatches leading to severe balance sheet effects of depreciations; capital structure mismatches with excessive reliance on debt relative to equity leading to lack of risk sharing and rigid external debt payment structures. Indeed, in 1997 short-term foreign currency debt was very high; forex reserves were extremely low especially after futile attempts to defend overvalued pegs; and the financing of current account deficits was mostly – Malaysia being one exception – in the form of debt rather than equity (FDI and portfolio inflows in equity markets) in part because of policy restrictions to inward FDI as in the case of Korea. Today, it looks like the opposite: short-term foreign currency debt has been sharply reduced; foreign exchange reserves are massive, providing a huge war chest against speculative attacks and being – if anything – a multiple of what is necessary based on prudent adequacy ratio; and FDI has been liberalized in Korea and the region so that massive amounts of FDI and portfolio inflows in equity markets are flowing into the region.

Third, in 1997 real capital investment was excessive (with investment rates very high as a share of GDP and hovering around 35 percent of GDP) and with low returns. Indeed, then firms in the region were trying to maximize size rather than the return to their capital leading to too much investment ('conspicuous size-maximizing investment'). Indeed, total factor productivity (TFP) growth was low if not negative as Paul Krugman popularized the results of academic studies on TFP in his famous 'Myth of the Asian Miracle' article. Government related policy distortions (implicit or explicit government bailout guarantees) increased moral hazard and led to excessive capital accumulation financed with short-term debt and foreign currency debt. Distortions and vulnerabilities in the corporate and financial systems were widespread with connected and directed lending being serious problems and corporate governance being weak and leading to excessive borrowing and excessive capital spending. Such high-and low-return investment rates were behind the large and growing current account deficits that eventually became unsustainable once the sudden stop of capital inflows occurred in mid-1997. Today, on the surface all looks different: investment rates have sharply fallen by about 10 percent of GDP (with China and Vietnam being an exception). While GDP growth rates are now lower than in 1997 they are only modestly so (about 2 percent below the roaring growth rates before the crisis), Thus, the return to investment is much higher (low incremental capital output ratios or high marginal returns to capital). Some of the reduction in potential and actual growth rates is structural: by achieving middle income (or even advanced economy in the case of Korea and the other NICs) status the income convergence from low per capita income has been vastly achieved; thus, potential growth must be lower than in earlier stages of economic development. Also, today corporate and financial sectors are much improved and banking and corporate restructuring and reforms – as well as much better corporate governance – have sharply reduced the financial vulnerabilities of the corporate, financial and banking system.

Fourth, in 1997 there was a lack or drought of liquidity as liquidity/rollover runs and low forex reserves led to severe liquidity crunches; such illiquidity of sovereigns, corporations, banks and financial intermediaries led to near-insolvency of many of these agents, a default risk that was at times triggered by illiquidity rather than true economic and financial insolvency. Such illiquidity forced countries to impose capital controls on outflows (Malaysia, Thailand) and/or more draconian suspension (followed by coercive restructuring) of debt payments to insolvent/illiquid corporates and financial institutions (Thailand, Indonesia, Korea) and it led these countries to rely on painful and austere IMF programs to deal with the massive liquidity runs and crunches. The runs followed by near insolvency, credit crunches and IMF imposed fiscal and monetary tightening led to falling economies (with severe recessions in 1998) in the midst of free-falling currencies, falling equity markets, falling housing values and sharply rising sovereign and non-sovereign bond and credit spreads. Today, it all looks like the opposite. Instead of a liquidity crunch we have if anything a slosh of excess liquidity as partially sterilized forex intervention and reserve accumulation is leading to easy monetary and credit conditions. Also, the excess of savings in Asia (with investment rates being much lower than savings rates) is keeping long-term nominal and real interest rates low, adding to the easy financial conditions in the global economy. Given the inflows of FDI and financial capital (some of it 'hot money'), countries in the region are now starting to think about controls on capital inflows, not outflows (see the recent case of Thailand and the recent Chang Mai debates on how to control excessive capital inflows). Given that now forex reserves are so large and self-insurance massive not only would these economies not need the IMF if downward financial pressures were to return; rather the IMF is obsolete in the region and the recent step to multilateralize the pooling of forex reserve (by now $80 billion of swap arrangements) and enhance regional surveillance in the context of the Chang Mai Initiative is creating the seeds of an Asian Monetary Fund, an idea that Japan proposed during the Asian crisis but that was then crushed by the US opposition to it. Thus, today instead of falling economies and collapsing financial markets we have sharply growing economies, rising currencies, sharply rising stock markets, housing values and other asset prices, and very low sovereign and corporate spreads. What a difference a decade has made!

Fifth, in 1997–1998 China, India and Japan were in trouble (while the other two BRICs, Brazil and Russia had their own severe financial crisis in 199 and 1999). China experienced its own version of a hard landing by 1998 when the Asian crisis led to a sharp economic slowdown to a low growth rate of 4 percent (4 percent being a hard landing for an economy like China). After letting its currency depreciate in 1995 and experiencing a surge in inflation the investment bubble of the early 1990s went into a bust and the Chinese economy sharply slowed down by 1998; it took repeated pleading by the US to convince China not to let its currency devalue during the Asian crisis and thus play a good citizen role and avoid further currency turmoil in Asia in the midst of the crisis. Japan was then in the midst of its economic and financial crisis: a chronic decade-long near recession, a semi-bankrupt financial and corporate system in bad need of restructuring, and serious price deflation, a very weak yen and massive yen carry trades. India was then barely recovering from its own financial crisis and emergency IMF rescue program of the early 1990s and, while it was not seriously affected by the East Asian financial crisis, it was only starting to implement its macro and structural reforms that led to a sharp increase in economic growth only in the current decade. Today, it all looks like the opposite: it is the decade of the BRICs and/or Chindia. China is booming and, if anything, suffering from overheating; India is rising and has emerged as a regional economic power that could one day rival China; Russia and Brazil have recovered from their own crises, are now growing fast and accumulating a massive amount of foreign reserves and even Japan is on the mend with corporate and financial restructuring now mostly achieved, the economic growth recovering and deflation possibly defeated. The one and only similarity to 1998 appears to be the resurgence of the weak yen and of the yen carry trades, an issue we will discuss in detail below.

So, leaving aside the yen carry trade, the world of 2007 in Asia looks on the surface as the opposite of the world of 1997: then economic and financial crises, severe financial vulnerabilities and free-falling markets; now booming economies and financial markets, reform and resolution of financial vulnerabilities and buoyant asset markets bordering on the bubbly.

Given the five structural differences between 1997 and 2007 is all clear for Asia? Are there no risks and vulnerabilities? I will now argue that Asia learned some of the lessons of its 1997–1998 financial crisis well addressing many of its own sources of vulnerabilities; but it has also learned some wrong lessons from that crisis and – in trying to address that crisis – planted the seeds of new and different financial vulnerabilities that could lead to a different crisis in the medium term, or even in the short term if global shocks such as US hard landing takesplace. Paradoxically, part of the policy responses to the 1997–1998 crisis were mistaken and created excessive liquidity and asset bubbles that will come to haunt the region once external shocks take place.

What are the problems with the current Asian economic, currency and financial model? The answer is, in brief, the effective return to fixed exchange rates in spite of the rhetoric of a move to floating rates. In other terms, the problem of Asia today is its membership of the Bretton Woods 2 (BW2) and the economic distortions, and financial and asset bubbles that this BW2 regime generates. Let me elaborate. After the 1997–1998 crisis, Asia only formally moved to a regime of flexible exchange rates. Effectively, instead, most countries in the region tried to avoid the appreciation of their currencies that had collapsed during the crisis, were thus severely undervalued and were thus subject to appreciating pressures once their economies and external balances recovered. Some of the attempt to prevent currency appreciation after 1999 was justified: these countries had gotten in trouble because of large and eventually unsustainable current account deficit and low stock of liquid foreign exchange reserves. So, once the external balances moved from a large deficit to a large surplus (given the collapse of imports during the 1998 recession and the sharp real depreciations during the crisis) the desire to accumulate forex reserves was fully justified as a form of self-insurance against future liquidity runs; these countries did indeed need a war chest of reserves as a buffer against potential future currency turmoil. Also, since currencies had been overvalued before the crisis and investment rates were excessive, the move from external deficits to external surpluses was – for a while – justified. In addition, keeping currencies undervalued for a while to build up forex reserves was also fine. There was thus a change in the Asian growth model, from a capital importing one with large current account deficits and reliance on domestic demand (investment and consumption) to a capital exporting one with export-led growth based on undervalued currencies, external surpluses and reliance on net exports and investment directed toward the production of tradables. That new model of growth was first and foremost chosen by China. Following the Chinese bandwagon most of the East Asian countries joined this BW2 model of fixed rates and undervalued currencies leading to export-led growth with current account surpluses and reserve accumulation attempting to prevent nominal and real appreciation.

As said above, the initial forex intervention was justified by the need to accumulate reserves and avoid the risk of new liquidity runs. So it was fully justified: during the Asian crisis the ratio of short-term foreign currency debt to forex reserves was well above one and closer to three or four in many economies; thus the risk of self-fulfilling liquidity runs was severe. However, by 2007 the reserve accumulation had become well above what was justified by prudent reserve adequacy ratios. In Korea in 1997 the ratio of short-term debt was close to a risky 500 percent; by 2007 that ratio was not only well below 100 percent (the threshold for the risk of liquidity runs) but closer to 20 percent. With reserves in many countries now four or five times the amount of short-term foreign currency debt (the opposite of 1997) reserve adequacy ratios are massively above any prudential criterion. For example if one had to use the Guidotti-Greenspan criterion of reserves being above short-term foreign currency debt, most countries in East Asia satisfy this criterion by an order of four or five times that prudential ratio.

So, what happened after 1998 was that the initial accumulation of forex reserves that was justified by the self-insurance needs gave way – especially after 2002 – to an accumulation of reserves solely explained by mercantilist objectives, i.e., the desire to keep currency values undervalued and pursue export-led growth, i.e., a growing membership of most of Asia into the new BW2 regime of effective fixed rates and weak currencies.

One may then ask: What is wrong with that BW2 growth model if it has led to high growth in China and East Asia and strong and well-performing financial and asset markets? The answer is clear.

First, this new economic and financial model is leading to excessive monetary and credit growth, asset bubbles in stock markets, housing markets and other financial markets that will eventually lead to a buildup of financial vulnerabilities – like the capital inflows and bubbles that preceded the Asian crisis of 1997 in a region of semi-fixed exchange rates – that could trigger a financial crisis different from that of 1997–1998 but that could be potentially as severe.

Second, reliance on an economic growth model based on rising growth of net external demand and domestic investment aimed at rising capacity for such exports; low reliance on domestic demand and production for domestic markets, especially private consumption and production of necessary non-tradable public and private services. This model of growth with excessive reliance on net exports and production of capacity for exports is dangerous for several reasons: it makes Asia – that used to rely in the 1990s on capital flows from the rest of the world for its growth – now reliant on US and global demand from outside Asia for its growth; given the current risks of a US hard landing or even a serious US growth slowdown this is a dangerous and vulnerable model of growth. Moreover, reliance on an ever-increasing level of next exports (both absolute and as a share of GDP) increases the risks of a protectionist backlash in the US and Europe. Thus, this export-led-only growth model is unsustainable and a more balanced growth pattern with greater reliance on domestic demand is essential to ensure long-run growth stability.

Let me elaborate on why the wholesale acceptance – with a few exceptions – of BW2 and of its related export-led growth model is dangerous for China, East Asia and the whole of the Asian continent. Notice also that many other economies outside of East Asia are following this BW2 regimes of fixed exchange rate, aggressive attempt to prevent appreciation via reserve accumulation and export-led growth. These include countries as far as India, Russia, Argentina, the GCC countries and other Middle East countries that are oil exporters and, until recently, even Brazil and other parts of Latin America. So the problems and financial vulnerabilities that we will outline below are relevant not just for East Asia but also for a broader group of emerging market economies around the world.

Paradoxically, the five factors discussed above – that apparently differentiate current conditions from those in 1997 – are partly not as different today from yesterday as some things have not changed compared to the conditions at the eve of the 1997 crisis and during the crisis period. Here are ten points and observation on how Asia has not learned the true lessons of the 1997–1998 crisis and how its policies are creating the basis of a future financial crisis in the region.

First, notice that BW2, fixed rates, easy monetary condition and low interest rates, asset bubbles and excessive reliance on export-led growth are all interconnected. Weak currencies, aggressive forex intervention to prevent appreciation in spite of current account surpluses and capital inflows lead to distorted relative prices – an undervalued real exchange rate – that punish domestic private consumption and production of productive non-tradable services and reward exports, investment for exportables and investment in non-directly productive real estate and housing.

Second, the move to flexible exchange rate after the 1997–1998 crisis was only temporary and soon these economies returned to effectively fixed or semi-fixed exchange rates in the new BW2 regime. Before the crisis the currency levels were somewhat overvalued; today they are grossly undervalued. Moreover, the attempt to prevent the necessary nominal and real appreciation of currencies – that are both undervalued and under appreciation pressure because of current account surpluses and net private capital inflows in the form of FDI, capital inflows in equity and bond market and hot money short-term inflows – is leading to a massive and unprecedented increase in forex reserves in all of Asia. By now the stock of forex reserves of the Asian economies is about $2.5 trillion ($2.28 trillion at the end of 2006) from its level of $250 billion in 1997, a tenfold 1000 percent increase in a decade. The growth of reserves in Asia was $251 billion in 2005 and a whopping $418 billion in 2007 based on recent ADB data and the growth of reserves has been accelerating in 2007. China used to accumulate reserves at a rate of an already huge $20 billion per month in 2006. In Q1 of 2007 that reserve accumulation has doubled to a per month rate of $40 billion. As the current account surplus increases, FDI rises, capital inflows in the equity market grow because of highly publicized IPOs of banks and other firms, and hot money inflows increase because of expectations of an appreciating RMB the need to accumulate reserve at a much faster rate is the necessary outcome. The Chinese central bank, that had already a serious problem in trying to sterilize reserves at a rate of $20 billion a month, is now facing a nightmare trying to handle and sterilize reserves at a monthly rate of $40 billion in Q1 of 2007.

Third, the ability of these economies to sterilize their forex reserve accumulation is severely limited. In China only between two-thirds and three-quarters of reserve accumulation is sterilized. In other countries in the region sterilization rates are also well below unity. Sterilization cannot be full for both practical and conceptual reasons: practically, money markets are not very well developed in many of these economies; so there are technical constraints to sterilization; banks are increasingly balking in China and other economies to hold low-yielding sterilization bonds when lending rates are much higher; thus, administrative actions such as higher reserve requirements or moral suasion have to be used by monetary authorities to induce the banks' acquisition of such sterilization bonds. This imposes further burden, taxes and distortions on the banking system. Finally, if sterilization was full and successful, nominal interest rates would not be reduced and instead stay higher than equilibrium, thus inducing further inflows of capital. Thus, successful sterilization would be self-defeating as only partial sterilization – by reducing domestic interest rates – would reduce the incentives of investors to move capital into these economies.

Fourth, partially sterilized intervention is leading to lower than equilibrium interest rates, massive growth in the monetary based and massive growth of bank lending and credit growth. China has been attempting to control credit growth and the ensuing investment and asset bubbles that it generates via administrative controls on credit and real investment. However, such controls are increasingly ineffective and source of further distortions in the allocation of savings to investment. Excessively low policy rates and short-term interest rates and the accompanying credit bubbles are now becoming pervasive throughout Asia, especially the effective members of BW2.

Fifth, these monetary and credit growth and easy financial conditions are leading to inflationary pressures in these economies. Since the real exchange rate is undervalued relative to its much appreciated equilibrium level there are only two ways via which the actual real exchange rate can appreciate towards the stronger equilibrium one: either a nominal exchange rate appreciation or via domestic inflation. Since in most countries – with Korea, Thailand and Indonesia being partial exception – the nominal appreciation is prevented, the real appreciation is often occurring via an increase in domestic inflation. Somehow puzzling, such rise in inflation has not been observed yet in China. The reasons are various: a very flexible labor market with an excess supply of cheap labor from rural areas; bumper crops keeping agricultural and food prices low, high manufacturing productivity, growth reducing unit labor costs, price controls on oil, energy and controlled public services, mismeasurement of housing inflation as increasing rent or rental cost of home ownership is not properly measured, but in other economies where labor markets are not as flexible and/or where energy subsidies have been phased out inflation is rising: both in BW2 economies in East Asia and among effective members of BW2 outside that region (specifically in India, Russia, Argentina, GCC countries and other Middle East countries, etc.).

Sixth, these monetary and credit growth and easy financial conditions are leading to asset price inflation, especially in countries like China where goods inflation is limited, but more generally among most BW2 economies. These asset bubbles take various forms.

In China easy money and credit first led to a real investment boom in housing and in tradable sectors. At the same time China experienced a housing price bubble as home prices rose rapidly. With an economy growing at a real rate of 10–11 percent and nominally at a rate of about 13 percent having nominal lending rates of about 6 percent is ridiculously low and implying very low real cost of borrowing for firms trying to invest. No surprise that the investment rate in China is now close to 50 percent with the returns to these investment being likely to be low and falling given the amount of overinvestment and duplication of capital spending project given the provincial level competition to attract investment and increase growth. Once the central government attempted to crack down on excessive capital accumulation of real capital, the excess liquidity and credit in the financial system led to outright asset bubbles, first in housing and then in the stock market.

In other BW2 economies, real investment has not surged as the fallout of the Asian financial crisis (falling rates of investment that had low returns) kept investment low as a share of GDP. Instead we have observed credit and asset bubbles.

Credit bubbles were behind the consumer credit card bubble and bust into a crisis in Korea. Credit bubbles have led to housing boom and near bubbles in many East Asian economies (as well as in India, Russia, the Middle East and parts of Latin America). Sharply rising home prices are observed in China, Hong Kong SAR, Taiwan POC, Thailand even if in some of them the recovery in home prices had occurred after sharp falls in the real price of homes during the Asian crisis.

Home price increases are much lower than the increase in equity prices. In the 1999–2006 period the average annual *real* (i.e., inflation adjusted) percentage increase in equity prices has been 14 percent in India, 10 percent in Korea, 7 to 10 percent in Singapore, Thailand, Malaysia, Hong Kong SAR, Taiwan POC. In China where stock prices where underperforming until 2006 the rise in stock prices has been spectacular in the last 12 months, more than doubling in one year. Given controls on corporate and housing investment the excess liquidity and credit is now going into the stock market characterized by a dangerous bubble. It is true that the recovery of the stock market in most of East Asia after 1999 represented a recovery from the sharp falls during 1997–1998, but the rate of increase in stock prices has accelerated in 2005–2007 in ways that appear not fully related to economic fundamentals.

Rather, easy credit has led to a massive surge in leveraged investments in stock markets in many of these economies. In China alone it is estimated that retail stock market investors – most clueless about the financial risks that they face – are now estimated to be over 100 million; day-trading of the type observed during the US dot.com bubble in the late 1990s are now common throughout Asia. Similar housing and stock market bubbles – and at times temporary busts – have been observed in India, Russia, Mid-East oil exporters, Argentina and other BW2 member countries. Of course, some of the increases in equity prices and in other asset prices are related to the much improved economic fundamentals, but there are now increasing signals of asset price overheating and bubble conditions, as recent episodes of stock market turmoil in China, India and the Middle East suggest.

Seventh, the fiscal and financial costs of forex accumulation and partial sterilization are increasing. In China where deposit rates and rates on sterilization bonds are artificially kept low the fiscal costs of accumulation of low-yielding reserves are shoved into the financial system that is forced to accumulate sterilization bonds yielding 2 percent or slightly more when lending rates are at least 6 percent or more; also to controls monetary growth required reserve ratios have been repeatedly increased all the way to 11 percent most recently. Between sterilization bonds and required reserves about 20 percent of assets of Chinese banks are held in low-yielding (about 2 percent average) assets. This is a severe cost for a still financially repressed financial system. In other countries where short-term policy rates are higher or high (Turkey, Brazil, India, Iceland, etc.), the negative carry on low-yielding reserve accumulation financed by higher-yielding sterilization bonds is serious.

In addition, the eventual fiscal cost of accumulating dollar reserves when the long-term nominal and real exchange rate will appreciate is massive. In the case of China, such capital losses would be now equal to $200 billion (about 10 percent of GDP) if the RMB were to appreciate 20 percent and could rise to as high as $600 billion in three years: the more China prevents its RMB appreciation the larger will be the stock of reserves (over $2 trillion by 2009 given current rates of accumulation) and the larger the necessary and eventually unavoidable nominal and real appreciation (as high as 30 percent in a matter of three years).

Thus, the eventual capital losses of remaining in the BW2 regime will be massive, both in absolute terms and as a share of GDP. Similar concerns about excessive reserve accumulation and capital losses are partly behind the tentative decision of Korea, Thailand and Indonesia to partly abandon BW2 and to allow their currencies to appreciate (more on this below).

Eighth, undervalued currencies and rising current account surpluses imply that Asia is excessively reliant on US growth and growth outside of Asia and too little on domestic demand. The situation is extreme for the case of China but common throughout East Asia. In China the current account surplus went from about $30 billion in 2002 to $230 billion in 2006, or from 2 percent of GDP to almost 9 percent. Net exports and a rising investment directed to increase the capacity to increase exports are the main drivers of economic growth. Consumption rates (as a share of GDP) are extremely low while savings and investment rates are excessively high (about 58 percent and 49 percent of GDP respectively currently).

Thus, while the US is the consumer of first and last resort with its spending well in excess of its income (leading to massive current account deficits), China is the producer of first and last resort with its spending well below its income (leading to massive current account surpluses). More importantly, via the trade with China, most of East Asia depends on net exports and on the health of the US economy as much as China does.

There is currently a myth in Asia that the rising amount of intra-regional trade is making the region less dependent on US growth and growth outside the region. As a recent ADB report and a recent IMF's WEO study suggest this is a myth. Intra-regional trade in Asia and especially East Asia has mushroomed in the last six years, but this has made the regions even more dependent – both structurally and cyclically – on US and outside growth. These studies show that the change pattern of trade in Asia is making Asia more dependent on trade with the US and the rest of the world. It used to be the case that East Asian economies were directly producing final goods for the US and Europe.

However, in the last six years the patterns of trade specialization has radically changed: now East Asia produces intermediate goods and raw materials exported to China (rather than exporting goods directly to the US and Europe) that then uses these resources to assemble final good that are exported to the US and Europe. Thus, in spite of the massive increase in intra-regional trade the dependence of China and East Asia on external trade and exports to US, Europe and the rest of the world has significantly increased rather than decreased. The idea that this intra-regional trade has led to greater domestic growth and greater insulation of Asia's growth from demand developments in the rest of the world is utterly wrong. China and East Asia is more dependent on US growth and growth outside Asia than ever before, both structurally and cyclically.

At the same time that China and Asia is becoming more dependent on US and EU growth, protectionist pressures are rising in the US and Europe as global imbalances are growing and Asia is actively resisting currency adjustment, starting with China. These protectionist threats are now seriously rising in the US Congress and even in the US executive power. Thus, risks of trade wars following the lack of currency adjustment are now rising.

Ninth, the currency and economic policies of China and East Asia have contributed – among many other factors – to unsustainable global current account imbalances whose rebalancing now risks becoming disorderly rather than orderly. Global imbalances have many causes and sources including – crucially – the low levels of US private and public savings, but China and Asia have had an important role in aggravating these unsustainable imbalances. In some sense it does not matter whether the excess of savings over investment (that is by definition equal to a current account surplus) in Asia is due to the BW2 regime of undervalued currencies; or it is due to the investment drought in East Asia after its 1997–1998 crisis (China being an exception to this low investment regime); or it is due to Bernanke's view of a global savings glut that is especially serious in China and East Asia; or it is due to the structural factors (lack of a social security and safety net; lack of credit markets where consumers can borrow to spend more) that keep savings rates high and consumption rates low in China. In reality a combination of these factors have led to the excess of savings over investment (or current account surpluses) in Asia and kept global interest rates lower than otherwise thus, inducing – in addition to the US fiscal deficits – housing investment bubbles and a rise in private consumption and fall in private savings that is behind the US current account deficit.

Tenth, the excessively easy monetary and credit conditions caused by BW2 and partially sterilized forex intervention, as well as low global nominal and real interest rates generated by this Asian excess of savings over investment have created conditions that exacerbated the excess of spending over income in the US and have fed global assets bubbles in a variety of risky assets, be it equities, credit spread, sovereign emerging market spreads, worldwide housing bubbles, commodity price booms. Low long-term interest rates (Greenspan's bond market conundrum) from excessive savings and low short interest rates given partially sterilized massive forex intervention together with the slosh of global liquidity that forex intervention, easy money in Japan and massive yen carry trade and excessive savings create excessive liquidity in the global economy that is behind the asset bubbles, credit boom, excessive leverage among private equity, hedge funds and other leveraged institutions that we are observing today. These excesses have led to an imbalance global economies where real (global current account imbalances and excessive global dependence on now fragile US growth) and financial imbalances (credit booms, risky leverage, and asset bubbles) are growing.

In summary, BW2 was always a disequilibrium for Asia and the global economy; but now from a stable disequilibrium is becoming an unstable one. Partially sterilized intervention is feeding risky credit and asset bubbles; undervalued currencies that are prevented from appreciating via massive and increased interventions are causing both goods and asset inflation and bubbles. Policies of export-led growth and undervalued currencies are causing growing global imbalances that are becoming unsustainable and increasing the dependence of China and Asia on a fragile and now faltering US economic growth as the risk of a US hard landing is rising. They are leading to excessive liquidity, asset bubbles and disequilibria not just in the region but also globally and they are increasing the risks of protectionism in the US and Europe. Thus, this economic growth model is unstable for China, for East Asia and for the world economy. A more balanced global economy requires greater domestic demand in China and Asia and smaller global imbalances.

Also, the contribution of China and Asia to this orderly global rebalancing requires several combined policies. First, China has to let its currency appreciate at a much faster rate; and if the RMB appreciates at a faster rate other Asian economies will allow their currencies also to appreciate at a faster rate as currently they are worried about unilateral appreciation and loss of competitiveness in case China does not move faster. Currency appreciation will increase imports, private consumption and lead to more investment and production in non-tradable services and less resources going into tradable exports. Thus, the lesson of the Asian crisis is that currencies should become more flexible, not less flexible.

Second, China and the rest of Asia has to stimulate domestic demand through a fiscal expansion and greater public investment in infrastructure that will help the recovery of private investment currently hampered by the lack of public investment infrastructures. Fiscal expansion would also allow China to counter any slowdown of demand pressures deriving from a faster currency appreciation. Such fiscal expansion and creation of a social security system and social safety net will also allow to creating the conditions that will lead to lower private saving and higher investment.

Third, greater financial liberalization and financial market liberalization and competition (including allowing foreign entry in domestic financial markets) will allow the development of a credit culture that will lead households to consume and spend more and a better allocation of massive savings to the right investment projects.

To achieve all this a more flexible exchange rate regime and greater currency flexibility is necessary in Asia and throughout Asia. The policy dilemma that China and Asia faces today is the classic Triffin's inconsistent trinity: no country can have fixed exchange rates, an independent monetary and credit policy and capital mobility with no capital controls. In China, in spite of formal capital controls, capital mobility is widespread as such controls on inflows are very leaky. Thus, China by trying to keep an effective currency peg (as the rate of currency crawl is at a snail's pace) has completely lost control of monetary and credit policy as interest rates are forced to be much lower than they should be given the overheating of the economy; and the desperate attempts of the Chinese to control the overheating via administrative controls on credit are failing given that excessive liquidity moves from controlled to uncontrolled sectors (from a boom in capex investment to a boom in housing investment; from a bubble in housing prices to a bubble in stock prices). The only solution to regain monetary and credit policy independence is to allow greater exchange rate flexibility. Similarly throughout Asia and among other BW2 members – India, Russia, the Middle East, Argentina – the same inconsistent trinity problems are emerging causing credit booms, economic overheating, goods inflation and asset bubbles.

As in the case of the Asian crisis where overheating, massive capital inflows, fixed exchange rates, credit booms and asset bubbles in equities and housing eventually led to financial imbalances before 1997 and an eventual crisis in 1997–1998, the seeds of the next financial crisis are being planted today in Asia and in the other parts of the unstable BW2 system. It is true that today – compared to 1997 some vulnerabilities are different: we have current surpluses, large stock of foreign reserves, low stocks of short-term foreign currency debts. Thus, a financial crisis coming from the unraveling of BW2 would not take the form – as it did in 1997 – of an external debt crisis. However, as in the 1995–1997 period, attempts to follow the US dollar and maintain fixed rates are feeding capital inflows, monetary creation and asset bubbles. It is easily forgotten that what triggered the Asian crisis were global conditions: then a strong dollar, a weak yen and carry trade that eventually unraveled; concerns about a global slowdown after 1995 and negative terms of trade shocks. This time around, as long as the US economy was growing at a good rate the stable disequilibrium of BW2 could be maintained, but the trigger for its unraveling is likely to be, as in 1996–1997, a change in global conditions external to Asia, specifically today the risk of a US hard landing as the housing recession is now spreading to the rest of the economy, creating a credit crunch and leading to a slowdown of private consumption.

As long as the US achieves a soft landing in 2007 the stable disequilibrium of BW2 can continue for a while longer, but a US hard landing (in the form of a growth recession or outright recession) will tip the BW2 disequilibrium from a stable one to an unstable one for many reasons.

First, a US hard landing would imply a sharp reduction of Chinese growth given the dependence of China on net exports and investment to produce exportables. Goldman Sachs estimates that a 1.5 percent reduction in US growth, say from 3.5 percent potential to 2 percent actual as in recent quarters, leads over time to a reduction in Chinese growth of 2 percent, say from 11 to 9 percent. If the US experiences a hard landing in the form of a growth recession rather than a soft landing (i.e., a growth rate of 0.5 percent rather than 2 percent for a few quarters) the US growth slowdown – relative to a potential of 3.5 percent – is 3 percent rather than 1.5 percent. Then this 3 percent US slowdown would lead to a Chinese slowdown of 4 percent, not 2 percent, from 11 to 7 percent. If the US were to experience a true hard landing in the form of an outright recession, say negative growth of 1 percent for a year, the US growth slowdown would be 4.5 percent (from 3.5 to 1 percent) that would translate in a growth slow-down in China of 6 percent, from 11 to 5 percent. Five percent growth for China would be equivalent to a hard landing and such growth slowdown in China would lead to a massive growth slowdown in East Asia and Asia overall given Asia's dependence on US growth via its trade in components, intermediate inputs and raw materials with China. Such a US hard landing would also have – via its effect on China – sharp downward effects on commodities demand and prices leading to painful growth slowdown among emerging market energy and other commodity exporters in Asia, Latin America, Africa and the Middle East. Even in the case of a US growth recession – rather than an outright recession – the slowdown in China, Asia and emerging markets would be serious given their direct and indirect dependence on US growth.

Second, a US hard landing of either type would not only lead to a painful growth slowdown in Asia and around the world; it would also undermine the basis of the BW2 regime. That regime in which China and Asia provide cheap goods to the US and, at the same time, the financing of the US current account deficit (a system of 'vendor financing') is stable only as long as Chinese and Asian growth can continue via ever-expanding net exports. The US hard landing undermines that key condition for vendor financing, a rise in US imports from China and Asia. Also, while US imports would fall in a US hard landing scenario the US current account deficit would not shrink as now net factor income payments in the US current account are negative and increasing (as the stock of foreign debt is rising and the interest payments on US liabilities rising). Thus, while until now a system of vendor financing was financing an increase in Asian exports to the US, a US hard landing would imply Asian to continue financing the increased US foreign debt and its factor income servicing rather than growing exports to the US. Thus, the willingness of Asia and other BW2 regime members to finance the US would be undermine at the time that downward pressures on the US dollar from the US hard landing lead to greater expected capital losses on holdings of dollar reserves and dollar assets.

Third, in a US hard landing protectionist pressures that are already high in a soft landing outlook would become severe with tensions on currency values turning into increasingly acrimonious trade conflicts and trade wars. In a US hard landing the US would want China to let the RMB appreciate even more that it is pressing for now; but in that lower growth environment where Chinese growth suffers even more, China would resist even more strongly further RMB appreciation. Thus, the outcome of this currency conflict would be a trade war between the US and China.

Fourth, a US hard landing would lead to the unraveling of the bubbly conditions in financial markets, of the credit booms and leveraged investments that fed Asian and global asset bubbles. Risk aversion would sharply rise and investors' confidence would sharply fall. In the spring of 2006 an inflation scare in the US led to sharp market turmoil in G7 equity markets and in emerging markets' financial markets. In February and March 2007 a growth scare in the US following the subprime carnage led to another episode of financial turmoil in G7 and emerging markets. Now, if instead of growth 'scare' we were to experience a real US growth 'downfall' that takes the form of a hard landing (either a growth recession or an outright recession) the consequences for financial markets and real economies would be severe. Economies would sharply slow down, financial markets and risky assets would be shaken, global imbalances would not shrink as both US imports and exports would fall with the slowdown in global growth, dollar weakness and currency tensions would increase, and the risks of a protectionist trade war would increase.

Economic fragilities, boom and busts in housing and policy weaknesses in the US are at the core of global economic imbalances that are leading to the risk of a US hard landing and a disorderly rebalancing of global imbalances; but it is also true that Asian currency and financial policies have fed such US imbalances creating a climate of global excess liquidity, low policy rates and easy monetary conditions (including easy money in Japan and massive yen carry trades), low global interest rates given the excess of savings over investment that have fed the US imbalances via an easy financing of the US fiscal deficits and the feeding of the US housing bubble, low private savings and consumption boom that is now under threat given the bust of the housing bubble.

In the meanwhile the Asian policies have both fed the US bubbles and imbalances and made Asian growth even more hostage to US economic growth. The entire Asian economic development for the last six years has been based on creating and feeding the US excesses that are now at risk of unraveling, a system of global imbalances that is now in danger of falling apart. In the short run, Asia can do little to resolve this fragile disequilibrium. If the US hard landing occurs in 2007 the consequences for China and Asia would be painful even if easing of fiscal and monetary conditions would allow the region to partially absorb the US shock.

However, even if this hard landing scenario is avoided and the US experiences a soft landing in which China and Asia will continue to growth a strong and sustained rates, it is in the medium-term interest of China and Asia to phase itself out of this unstable BW2 and create conditions that allow greater dependence on domestic demand for growth rather than excessive reliance on net exports and being hostage to US growth. This change in the

Asian growth model requires a more sophisticated understanding of the lessons of the crisis of 1997–1998. It requires a true move to flexible exchange rate with resources relatively moving out of traded sectors into non-traded services, fiscal stimulus, greater public investment infrastructure spending, creation of social safety nets and greater financial sector liberalization, development and deepening that will allow households to spend more and smooth shocks to consumption from income and terms of trade volatility, and a better allocation of the vast amounts of Asian savings to greater real investments that will allow higher potential and actual growth and a more balanced type of growth that is a little less dependent on a volatile global economy.

The key to this rebalancing of Asian growth is a faster rate of appreciation of the RMB, greater currency flexibility in China and the ensuing generalized appreciation of Asian currencies relative to the US dollar once China allows a greater appreciation of the RMB. Until recently most Asian economies have been wary to allow their currencies to appreciate too much because of the persistent Chinese policy to maintain an effective RMB peg with a very small and slow rate of upward crawl.

Most Asian economies realized that maintaining an effective peg to the US dollar (or equivalently to the RMB) is costly: it leads to excessive forex reserve accumulation with its ensuing short-run fiscal costs and long-run large capital losses; it leads to excessive monetary growth – via partial sterilization – and credit booms that feed asset bubbles. Thus, there is increasing Asian economies' uneasiness with staying inside BW2, but as long as China keeps on pegging its currency most Asian economies can ill afford to get off the BW2 unstable train as the loss of competitiveness of their currencies relative to the RMB, relative to the other Asian currencies and relative to the G7 currencies would be serious and cause a loss of competitiveness and growth.

A few countries tried to get off the BW2 regime given the current and expected costs of staying in this regime and accumulating a dangerous stock of excessive forex reserves: these are Korea, Thailand and Indonesia that allowed a some significant appreciation of their currencies in the last few years. Some of this appreciation was necessary and not painful. These countries currencies had massively depreciated in real terms during the 1997–1998 crisis well beyond the lower equilibrium real exchange rate. The ensuing real appreciation that was unavoidable after the end of the crisis and return to external surpluses required a nominal appreciation that was allowed to prevent the process of real appreciation to occur through higher inflation, but the process of nominal appreciation in these economies continued and became excessive after this nominal appreciation was allowed since capital inflows to the region kept on surging.

Thus, these economies are facing a tough dilemma. A return to massive forex intervention is costly and feeds credit and asset bubbles, but allowing currencies to appreciate more leads to a significant loss of competitiveness. The outcome for Korea is particularly painful as the large appreciation of the won (over 25 percent relative to the Yen) is leading to a loss of competitiveness and slower growth (that is crawling down to about 4.5 percent recently). In Thailand a similar massive appreciation of the baht occurred in 2005–2006. To avoid excessive appreciation that would hurt growth Thailand tried to impose capital controls on inflows at the end of 2006, controls that were botched and led to a sharp fall in the Thai equity market. In Indonesia an appreciation took momentum and led to similar concerns about excessive appreciation. The dilemma faced by countries such as Korea, Thailand and Indonesia that are trying to jump off the BW2 train are painful: allow excessive appreciation and cause an excessive slowdown of growth; rejoin BW2 and keep on accumulating again reserves thus feeding credit and asset bubbles; trying to control inflows and appreciation through capital controls on inflows that may become counterproductive as are perceived as market unfriendly by domestic and foreign investors. Similar trade-offs are faced by Brazil that, for a while joined BW2 and then, like Korea, got off this system in 2006.

At the same time other East Asian economies such as Hong Kong, Taiwan, Singapore, Malaysia – as well as members of BW2 as far as India, Russia, Middle East/GCC, Argentina – have decided so far to stick with BW2, in Asia because China is still shadowing the US dollar and these economies in East Asia think they can ill afford to allow a loss of competitiveness of their currencies relative to the RMB given their direct and indirect trade links with China. However, this continued membership of BW2 is leading to a continuation of the imbalances and financial vulnerabilities generated by BW2.

These policy dilemmas and tensions will remain as long as China decides to remain the leading economy of this BW2 and maintains its effective peg to the US dollar (as the rate of upward crawl of the RMB is extremely small and slow); but these economic and financial imbalances and vulnerabilities generated by BW2 are serious and building over time increasing the risks of a new and different type of financial crisis in Asia once the unraveling of BW2 becomes disorderly rather than orderly.

Thus, even leaving aside the risks of protectionism in the US, it is of tantamount importance that China realizes that its exchange rate regime is creating economy and financial instability in its own economic and creating serious problems for its trading partners in Asia. Thus, China should realize that an orderly but rapid phase-out of BW2 is in its own national interest as it will allow – together with other complementary fiscal and financial policies – the achievement of a Chinese economic soft landing and rebalancing of its economic growth model in the direction of a more stable dependence on consumption and domestic demand. It will also allow Asia to develop a growth model where growth of intra-Asian trade makes the region less dependent – rather than more dependent – on the whims of uncertain US and EU growth and economic policies, including trade policies and their responses to the challenges of globalization.

9　Asia future currency arrangements

The Indonesian view

*Miranda Goeltom**

Background

Interest in regional currency arrangements and their theoretical foundation has surged for some time. The implementation of a monetary union has been initiated by the European Area over decades but the result has proven its success. The success of the euro has encouraged similar consideration in regions around the world and individual countries are exploring whether to join an existing monetary union or start a new one.

Included in this direction is the Arabian Gulf. The six countries of the Gulf Cooperation Council – Bahrain, Kuwait, Oman, Qatar, Saudi Arabia, and United Arab Emirates – are forming a monetary union with a single currency to be launched in 2010. In the West African zone, five countries, Ghana, the Gambia, Sierra Leone, Guinea, and Nigeria are forming the West African Monetary Zone which will issue the common currency, the 'eco' by 2010. In Southern Africa, the sixteen-member South African Development Community, led by South Africa, is planning a free trade area by 2008, a custom union by 2010, a common market by 2015, and a monetary union by 2016.

Similarly to other regions, the five South East Asian countries (Indonesia, Malaysia, Thailand, Singapore, and the Philippines) established ASEAN Free Trade Area in 2003. This is an important part of the larger process toward ASEAN Vision 2020[1] which is then accelerated to become an ASEAN Economic Community by 2015, covering the whole ten countries of ASEAN. The ASEAN cooperation is also widened to include another three important East Asian Countries, namely Japan, South Korea, and China, known as ASEAN+3.

The issue on economic and financial integration in East Asian countries resurfaced because of the financial crisis in 1997. The lessons from the crisis have spurred awareness to adopt preventive measures both at national and regional levels. While countries are strengthening their policies and institutional framework at regional level, self-help initiatives and support systems have been implemented and closer cooperation is enhanced among the countries in East Asia, in view of the limited resources available at global institutions and the need to establish better policy coordination among countries in the region.

Furthermore, the growing awareness of the need for stability in the region encourages continued measures toward economic and financial integration. In ASEAN, this economic and financial integration is drawn upon as an architecture consisting of two major economic and financial pillars as shown below (Figure 9.1).

It implies that exchange rate or currency arrangement is one of the important elements toward economic and financial integration in the region. Currency arrangement will facilitate and promote intra-regional trade and deepening regional economic integration as well as attaining regional financial stability. The question is whether the East Asia region is ready for adopting a currency arrangement in consideration of the different stage of economic development among countries and infrastructural aspects. A crucial precondition for a successful currency arrangement is the attainment of an optimum currency area (OCA), which is a geographical region in which it would maximize economic efficiency to have the entire region share a single currency. Countries in East Asia still differ in their readiness

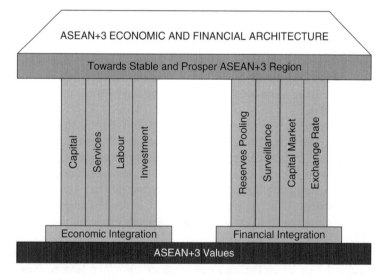

Figure 9.1 The architecture of economic and financial integration in East Asia.
Source: Asian Development Bank, 2005.

for OCA, which implies the need to strengthen their policies both at domestic and regional level.

In spite of this, the development in the East Asia region seems to continue to be heading toward further integration. This brings the need for further consideration on the future currency arrangement within the region and the steps that should be taken.

East Asia currency arrangement

The need for currency arrangement arises from the desire of a region to move toward closer economic and monetary integration. The choice by countries to undertake regional integration initiatives could be driven by economic, political, and social motives. From an economic perspective, the decision to pursue closer integration with a region rests on the belief that prospects for improving the standards and quality of living or elevating defense against economic and financial crises are brighter when countries get together compared to a unilateral pursuit of their own national interests.

There are two approaches on economic and monetary integration theories. The theory put forward by Bela Balassa (1961) states that 'trade follows financial', i.e. increase in trade will be followed by an increase in the financial sector. On the other hand, Herber Dieter (2000) states the other way 'financial follows trade', i.e. financial integration will increase regional trade intensity.

According to Bela Balassa (1961), economic and financial integration comprises five stages, namely: (i) free trade area, (ii) custom union, (iii) common market, (iv) economic union, and (v) total economic integration. Meanwhile, Herbert Dieter (2000) claims that economic financial integration comprises of only four stages, namely: (i) regional monetary fund, (ii) regional monetary system, (iii) economic and monetary union, and (iv) political union.

We can see that both theories imply the need for a regional monetary system, which would not materialize without an agreed currency arrangement within the region. There are three possible arrangements that could form the basis for a cooperative exchange rate arrangement in East Asia, namely: a single currency peg, a parallel currency, and currency basket arrangement. Under a single currency peg, the participating countries, would agree to jointly peg the currencies to either a major currency or a regional currency, or even a synthetic currency. A parallel currency is a synthetic currency existing in tandem with a national currency. The currency basket arrangement entails the management of the exchange rate against a common basket of currencies with the aim of managing the nominal exchange rate to keep fluctuation of the common basket index within a band.

Alternatively, given the diversity of Asian economies, a practical approach toward a common currency goal would first be through the clustering of small optimal currency areas, followed by the enlarging (or merging) of such clusters at a later stage.

The arguments for and against entering a currency arrangement with another country have been extensively studied in the academic literature. In broad terms, the key issue is whether the potential advantages of joining, in terms of greater macroeconomic stability and lower trade transactions costs, outweigh the loss of discretion to use monetary and exchange rate policies to respond to domestic and external shocks. In weighing these potential advantages and disadvantages, a number of the literature has identified several conditions that, if fulfilled, may boost the benefits and hence the long-term sustainability of a country's participation.

An important consideration for a region to establish a currency arrangement is the achievement of an optimum currency area (OCA). The classical theory of OCA was developed by Mundell (1961), as early as the 1960s known as the 'Theory of Optimum Currency Areas'. This theory focuses on criteria to be fulfilled for a country to join an OCA. These include, among others; (i) openness to the area members, (ii) product, factor, and financial market integration, (iii) symmetry of shocks affecting the area members, (iv) similarity of preferences over output-inflation trade-offs, and (v) willingness to coordinate supporting policies such as fiscal transfers.

The question is whether East Asia is already suitable as an optimum currency area. Eichengreen (2005) added another four preconditions that should be fulfilled by the Asia region to achieve monetary union. The OCA preconditions mentioned above are considered necessary but not sufficient to establish an OCA in the Asia region. These additional preconditions are: (i) the ability to delegate monetary policy to a credible supranational institution, (ii) transparent monetary policy, (iii) open capital account regime, and (iv) convergent monetary policy transmission mechanism. Furthermore, Bayoumi *et al.*, (1999) conclude that the Asian region principally has close similarity with the European region in meeting OCA criteria. However, the essential precondition establishing a sustainable regional cooperation actually lies in political factors rather than economic factors and Asian political factors are significantly different from those of the European region. This political commitment still appears to be difficult for Asia in the short run.

Further analysis also indicates that a currency arrangement in East Asia is yet to be applicable at the current state due to three factors:

1. There are high potential risks that may well outweigh the benefits. The risks include: risk for exchange rate misalignment considering the

ASEAN region is subject to asynchronous cycle and possibility of shocks; and risk of conflict between individual countries' domestic and regional interests in achieving the final goal of currency arrangement, taking into account the remaining lack of political commitment and heterogeneous nature of economic and financial systems within the region.

2. Due to the high potential risks mentioned above, the framework for currency arrangement is predicted to be non-sustainable.

3. A number of preconditions for currency arrangements are not yet fulfilled at the current juncture. These preconditions include: stronger political commitment, higher levels of regional economic, macroeconomic and financial convergence to ease policy coordination, a strong and independent supranational body, comprehensive macroeconomic surveillance, and regional financing arrangement

To materialize a strong currency arrangement in the future, the best action plan for East Asia is to work for enhanced integration and get ready for a more coordinated currency arrangement. A number of steps can be taken, including:

a. *Eliminating all trade barriers for intra-regional trade for both goods and services, and setting a clear time frame to reach a common market.* The following should be noted:

- ASEAN countries should focus more on finalizing various trade agreements among countries in the region aiming to increase intra-regional trade activities.
- Cluster system approach (multi-speed) proposed by ADB can be considered
- Revisiting the current implementation of 'spaghetti approach' (where each ASEAN country conducts trade agreements with countries outside the region) to allow for benefits for the region as a whole.
- To reduce the cost of trade transaction, the region should harmonize standards and regulations, enhancing the mobility of the production factor, and widening the transportation network between countries within the region as well as infrastructure related to the needed development of the real and financial sector.
- A range of efforts to remove trade barriers and integrate the trade sector should be accompanied by a blueprint to map out all trade agreements within the region.

b.   *Establishing a strong and credible supranational institution.* This institution is necessary to implement the various initiatives, much like the European commission. The institution should be given a full mandate and support both financially and politically from each member.
c.   *Enhancing a peer surveillance process in the regional level.* It is necessary to consider the approach taken by OECD in implementing country surveillance, where there is a permanent secretariat headed by two countries undertaking the surveillance process on a rotation basis.
d.   *Proceeding with measures to develop and integrate financial market.* ASEAN needs to enhance its development agenda related to infrastructure development both in the real and financial sector. In the financial sector, ASEAN could establish a regional fund or pool of regional expertise to assist each country in developing a financial sector infrastructure in the region.

Studies on currency arrangement

Many of the literature have discussed the possibility of ASEAN+3 countries becoming a regional currency arrangement. A study conducted by Singo Watanabe and Masanobu Ogura (2006) found that in Asia it is difficult to define homogeneous regions, as they tend to be pluralistic. There are significant differences in developmental stages among Asian countries. Such differences, arising partly from structural uniqueness of individual Asian countries, might affect the prioritization of their policy objectives. Moreover, there are variations in macroeconomic policy track records in Asia. The recent crisis has encouraged improved macroeconomic policy management by countries in Asia. Asian countries have re-built their economies according to the specific priorities of each country. In this situation, there may be little incentive to give up their monetary sovereignty for the sake of a currency union.

Furthermore, Watanabe and Ogura also state that there are no central bodies in place to design and promote the integration process, such as the European Commission and the Council of the Euroepan Union (EU). ASEAN is only a first step in terms of the Balassa sequencing. The Chiang Mai Initiative (CMI), a regional financial arrangement for East Asia, can be seen as just a further step toward a higher level of institutional regional integration. Furthermore, in Asia, the political and economic regimes as well as the levels of nominal and real convergence are more heterogeneous than in Europe. Political leadership and single-mindedness provide a strong background for integration in Europe and this does not seem to be present in ASEAN or the larger Asian region at the current time.

Therefore, the benefits of monetary integration would be lower and the associated costs and risks would be higher on this continent.

A deeper look into the OCA criteria with respect to development in Asia indicates that there has been a degree of progress toward integration:

1. *Intensity of intra-region trade.* Statistical data of export and imports of countries in the region indicates that intra-regional trade in East Asia has significantly increased within the last decade. The contribution of the region to individual countries' total trade has also shown an increase. In 2004, this contribution reached 45 and 69.8 percent for export and import respectively from 40.1 and 51.7 percent in 2000. Moreover, the role of plus three countries has increased the intensity of intra-ASEAN+3 trade quite significantly. The share of intra-ASEAN+3 countries to total trade of the region has increased from 33.9 and 38.9 percent (exports and imports) in 1995 to 37.3 and 45 percent in 2004.

2. *Symmetrical shock.* This criterion analyzes the pattern of economic shock within a region (symmetrical or asymmetrical) in order to determine to what extent a region is heading toward economic convergence. This pattern of shock and its implications can be seen from a number of angles, among others level of income, economic structure, trade composition and trading partners, correlation with business cycle, level of similarity among countries and aggregate and supply. From the level of income, the East Asia region is still facing a high level of income disparity, while from the economic structure and characteristic, countries in East Asia region generally differ due to the different natural resources available and the differences of sectoral contribution to the formation of GDP. From the trade composition and trading partners, recent development indicates that export product composition varies between one group of countries and another within the region. Moreover, despite increasing in East Asia intra-trade, the US and Europe are still the major trading partners for countries in the region.

3. *Compensating adjustment mechanism.* This criterion analyzes the current condition whether an adjustment mechanism alternative is available in the region once member countries agree to form fully-fledged economic integration. There are three alternatives for adjustment mechanisms, namely: (i) price and wages flexibility, (ii) factor mobility – in particular labor, and (iii) fiscal transfer. In terms of price and wage flexibility, the labor market in East Asia is becoming more regulated after the signing of the International Labor Organization Convention. This is reflected among others in the application of minimum wages in each country, and establishment of workers' unions. Consequently, the labor market in East Asia tends to be less flexible in adjusting for

shocks in the region. In terms of factor mobility, the region is characterized by migration of low-skilled labor from poorer countries to the
wealthier ones. This may lead to the potential of social problems and
political tension between the supplier and recipient countries. The low
quality of labor will result in ineffective labor mobility.

4. *Maastricht nominal convergence criteria.* This is criteria which is set by
    the European Community to achive monetary union. The comparison of
    East Asian countries' condition during 2000–2005 using Maastricht
    criteria shows that countries in the region have not fully met the
    Maastricht threshold, which implies that monetary policies in the regional
    perspective to respond to shock in the region would not be effective.

Indonesia has also conducted thorough studies on the subject of ASEAN
currency arrangement. The study (Suseno *et al.*, 2006) covers the readiness
of ASEAN+5 countries (Indonesia, Malaysia, Thailand, the Philippines,
Singapore) based on indicators of preconditions for a single currency in the
region and ASEAN convergence in attaining certain targets such as inflation,
economic growth exchange rate and fiscal convergence.

The study on preconditions to formation of a single currency, using both
pairwise and multi-variate methods, finds that countries that are currently
having a bigger chance to form a single currency are Singapore, Malaysia
and Thailand. Multi-variate models with hierarchical clustering models show
that Singapore, Malaysia, and Thailand are in one cluster, whilst Indonesia
and the Philippines are in another. When one looks deeper at individual
conditions for the forming of a single currency, it seems that many conditions are not yet fulfilled by Indonesia and the Philippines relative to the
other three ASEAN+5 countries, namely Singapore, Malaysia, and Thailand.
Each cluster presents similar characteristics such as per capita income, inflation correlation, symmetry of shocks, ratio of investment to GDP, ration of
agriculture and services sector value added to GDP.

To examine whether ASEAN+5 or ASEAN+3 (Singapore, Malaysia,
Thailand) is economically converged, convergence analysis was conducted
using two methods, namely β-convergence and γ-convergence. The
outcomes of convergence analyses showed that per capita income in
ASEAN+5 and ASEAN+3 is not converged. This implies that underdeveloped economies have to grow faster than the developed ones and that
economic dispersion has to become narrower.

Subsequently, Maastricht criteria (indicators) are also used to analyze
economic convergences among ASEAN countries. The outcomes show that
not all indicators are converged. For ASEAN+5 analysis, four out of five
criteria are converged, i.e. inflation, budget deficit, exchange rate, and interest rate. In the meantime, for ASEAN+3 analysis, four out of five indicators

can be converged, namely inflation (2.9 years), budget deficit (3.5 years), exchange rate (15.2 years), and interest rate (3.5 years). This verifies that ASEAN+5 and ASEAN+3 are still yet to fulfill all Maastricht criteria, particularly for the debt-to-GDP ratio indicator.

Other Indonesian research on the possibility of establishing economic integration in the ASEAN+3 area was conducted by Achsani and Siregar (2006). The analysis takes into account all ten ASEAN member countries plus three other Asian countries, i.e. China, Japan, and South Korea. The study examines the degree of economic and financial integration among ASEAN+3 countries by using daily data of the stock composite main index in each country and then comparing the results with that which has been done in the European Union. Using the correlation and VAR analyses, the results show that the countries in the region are not yet fully integrated. In terms of the financial market, China is still isolated from other ASEAN+3 countries. The level of financial integration between North-east and South-east Asia is also relatively low. Their findings also suggested that the economic structures of the ASEAN members itself could be classified into at least three clusters: core member (Singapore, Malaysia, Thailand, Indonesia, the Philippines, and Vietnam), less developed members (Myanmar, Cambodia, and Laos), and developed member (Brunei).

Indonesia's strategy for joining an Asian currency arrangement

From Indonesia's perspective in particular, a number of steps and policies have currently been taken to meet the preconditions of OCA. These include policies on labor, monetarism and finance, international trade, and the fiscal, and real sector.

Labor policy

On the labor front, there is a need to increase flexibility in wages within the ASEAN+5 countries. Wages flexibility is considered important as an instrument to counter asymmetric shocks. Furthermore, efforts should be taken to enhance labor and capital mobility within the ASEAN+5 countries to respond to asymmetric shock problems as well as to reduce the need for nominal exchange rate adjustment. However, it is worth noting that the pace of recommendations mentioned above depends on individual countries' economic and social conditions.

For Indonesia, labor policy has moved on the right track toward increasing labor mobility. This is reflected in the National Medium-term Development Plan 2004–2009, which states that the direction of labor sectors are: (i) creating as wide as possible formal or modern work opportunities, and (ii) giving necessary support such that labor can move from one job having low productivity to another with higher productivity. Furthermore, the National Long-term Development Plan 2005–2025 was also established to increase (i) the creation of formal work opportunities as widely as possible, and (ii) welfare of labor in the informal sector.

Monetary and financial policies

With respect to financial policy, developing financial markets in each member country such as developing bond and equity markets is needed. This development is needed to make financial market structures non-reliant solely on the banking sector. A robust and stable financial market is vital for a country to absorb economic shocks.

As regards monetary policy, it is important to maintain one country's level of inflation not significantly different from others, particularly countries having an inflation benchmark (low and stable inflation). It is important for Indonesia and the Philippines to manage their level of inflation since levels are structurally higher than the other three ASEAN+5.

There is also a need to increase external sustainability in reserves and net foreign assets. ASEAN member countries need to maintain net foreign assets and reserves at the same level since this would make it easier for the ASEAN countries to use the same monetary policies in the aim to reduce the negative impact of asymmetric shocks.

For Indonesia, up until now, monetary and financial policies are on the right track, meaning it adopts a prudent monetary policy and strengthened financial sector stability to reduce inflation and maintain exchange rate stabilization. Unfortunately, Indonesia's monetary and financial policies are still facing several odious obstacles and challenges as reflected in the following conditions: (i) vulnerable macroeconomic stability towards external shocks, (ii) high inflation and interest rate as compared with other countries in the region, (iii) real sector that has not fully recovered and some flaws in the banking sector, and (iv) low capital market's role as a source of long-term funds for the private sector.

International trade policy

On the international trade front, there is a need to enhance trade cooperation among ASEAN+5 countries, in particular intra-industry trade to reduce asymmetric shocks. Moreover, it is encouraged to increase relative economic openness among these countries with regard to increased intra-ASEAN trade. Measures to increase intra-industry trade are among others: (i) increase foreign direct investment as the main channel for strengthening intra-industry trade since it will strengthen network production, (ii) enlarge technological know-how, (iii) raise trade liberalization, (iv) set port and custom standardization, (v) improve logistics cost and supply chain structure to strengthen network production and increase member countries' competitiveness, and (vi) enhance entrepreneurship as an important condition for the innovation process.

Policy measures taken in Indonesia are obvious in enhancing international trade, particularly in economic openness as well as product and market diversification. In the National Medium-term Development Plan 2004–2009, it is clearly stated that policies in the international trade sector are to increase and broaden international market access as well as strengthen the performance of exporters and candidate exporters. These are achieved, among others, through: (i) encouraging gradually the broadening of export product base, (ii) gradually increasing export value-added, (iii) revitalizing the performance of export promotion institutions and strengthening small exporters training institution capacity, and (iv) increasing improved performance of international trade diplomacy.

In the National Long-term Development Plan 2004–2025, it is stated that international trade is directed toward supporting the Indonesian economy so that it can reap maximum benefits as well as minimize the negative effects of integration and globalization. Several measures are achieved through: (i) strengthening the national position in various international trade fora (global, regional, bilateral), and (ii) developing national image, product and services standard and facilitating competitive international trade.

Indonesia, as a matter of fact, has much potential to increase trade among the ASEAN+5 member countries for the following reasons: (i) its exports are still highly dependent on three traditional markets – namely the US, Japan, and Singapore, (ii) increased non-tariff barriers, particularly from developed countries, (iii) potential increase in export product uniformity, and (iv) less optimal on incentives and facilities for exports mainly for small and medium exporters.

Fiscal policy

There is a need for a strengthened fiscal transfer mechanism as an instrument to reduce the need for exchange rate adjustment. Countries having a similar fiscal transfer system are allowed to transfer funds to other member countries experiencing negative transfer. Furthermore, each member country should maintain its level of budget deficit since one of the OCA preconditions is a low level of budget deficit.

Indonesia's fiscal policy until now is on the right track as it reduces budget deficit to a low level. Furthermore, medium- and long-term policy directions make clearer the current policies. In the National Medium-term Development Plan 2004–2009, it is clearly stated that policies in the fiscal sector are directed toward, among others: (i) balancing increased budget allocation with an effort to strengthen fiscal sustainability, (ii) increased government revenue through tax and custom policy and administration reform, (iii) increasing effectiveness and efficiency of government expenditure, and (iv) enhanced management of government foreign debts aiming to reduce foreign debt stocks to GDP in relative and absolute terms.

However, one should be mindful that Indonesia's prudent fiscal policy focusing on fiscal sustainability faces odious challenges brought about by: (i) high poverty and unemployment rate, (ii) unrecovered real sector from crisis, (iii) high debt burden, and (iv) various external shocks such as world oil price and natural disasters.

Real sector policy

In the real sector, there is a need to increase investment flexibility in each member country. Increased investment flexibility is needed to facilitate an increase in intra-industry trade. Such an increase is closely related to efforts to increase foreign direct investment, and this is achieved through reducing barriers to investment procedures in each member country in order to attract foreign investors.

Progress on Indonesia's real sector policy concerning the increase in investment flexibility is quite impressive, particularly policies related to efforts to elevate foreign direct investment. In the National Medium-term Development Plan 2004–2009, it is stated that enhancing government investment will be focused on: (i) reducing transaction costs and high cost economy for initial stages as well as operational stages, (ii) ensuring business certainty and strengthening law enforcement, guaranteeing property rights, and equal treatment on settlement dispute mechanism, (iii) improving investment policy in accordance to best international practices such as non-discrimination treatment between foreign and domestic investors, an incentive system in investment policy, and investment institution reforms, and (iv) improving harmonization between central and regional regulations.

In the National Long-term Development Plan 2005–2025, it is stated that Indonesian investment policy is directed toward supporting the attainment of sustainable high and qualified economic growth through materializing an attractive investment climate, encouraging foreign investment with the aim of increasing national economic competitiveness, and enhancing physical infrastructure capacity.

Investment policy in Indonesia, as a matter of fact, still faces big challenges due to: (i) an increase in competitiveness between countries to grasp investment, (ii) high license and operational costs in Indonesia, (iii) weak law enforcement, and (iv) unsound incentive systems.

Closing remark

Economic integration among the ASEAN+3 economies has gained momentum in the previous decade. The Asian financial crisis proved to be a driving force behind this phenomenon. It highlighted how the regional economic landscape has changed, and opened the idea that more integration is beneficial for East Asia. Various measures have been taken in the path of achieving stronger economic and financial integration in the region.

One of the important pillars toward economic integration is monetary integration among the ASEAN+3 economies. The region is still a long way off a monetary union. One of the indications is that the region as a whole is still lacking in fulfilling the OCA criteria. The ASEAN+3 countries should be an OCA in order to succeed in adopting a common exchange rate policy. At the same time, there still exist a number of difficulties in adopting a common exchange rate policy among them because the countries have different stages of economic development and lack of political commitment.

However, some academic literature on this topic concurs that the optimal currency area conditions seem to be met by 'subsets' of Asian countries, although the ultimate success of an Asian currency union hinges crucially on such factors as historical and political backgrounds, robustness of institutional set-ups, degree of regional convergence in development states, and the track record of sound macroeconomic policy in constituent countries. In this regard countries in the region could be divided into clusters, each consisting of countries with similar characteristics based on certain criteria.

To materialize a strong currency arrangement in the future, the best action plan for East Asia is to work for enhanced integration and get ready for a more coordinated currency arrangement. A number of steps can be taken, including eliminating all trade barriers for intra-regional trade for both goods and services, and setting a clear time frame to reach a common market, establishing a strong and credible supranational institution, enhancing peer surveillance processes at the regional level, and proceeding with measures to develop and integrate financial markets.

As in other ASEAN countries, Indonesia's agenda is still to be taken to meet the preconditions of OCA. These include policies on labor, monetarism and finance, international trade, and the fiscal and real sectors. The efforts to strengthen Indonesia's readiness to meet OCA and further keep up with the process of economic and financial integration should include (i) gaining political commitment from the government, (ii) increasing coordination among related institutions, both public and private, (iii) optimizing regional and international cooperation to strengthen the domestic economy, (iv) establishing a national roadmap for domestic industry, both in the real and financial sector, (v) enhancing national surveillance effectiveness, and (vi) strengthening and completing supporting infrastructure in trade, investment and international financial transactions.

Notes

* Paper presented by Dr. Miranda S. Goeltom at Seminar on a Decade Later: Asia New Responsibilities in the International Monetary System. Seoul. Korea, May 2–3, 2007
1 The ASEAN 'Vision 2020' was initiated by heads of government in ASEAN during the ASEAN Summit in Kuala Lumpur on 15 December 1997 to further economic cohesion or integration as a long-term response to the crisis. This statement was soon followed by an action plan concluded in 1998 at the ASEAN Summit in Hanoi, which, among other things, called for a strengthening of the financial system in the region.

Bibliography

Achsani, Noer Azam, and Hermanto Siregar (2006). *Financial and Economic Integration: Experience of the EU and Future Prospect for ASEAN+3*. Department of Economics, Bogor Agricultural University, Indonesia.

Arifin, Sjamsul, R. Winantyo, and Yati Kurniati (ed.) (2007). *Financial and Monetary Integration in East Asia*. Bank Indonesia, 2007.

Asian Development Bank (2005). *Asian Economic Cooperation and Integration: Progress, Prospect and Challenges*. ADB: Manila, 2005.

Balassa, Bela (1961). *The Theory of Economic Integration*. Homewood, Illinois: RD Irwin, 1961.

Bayoumi, Tamim, Barry Eichengreen, and Paulo Mauro (1999). *On Regional Monetary Arrangements for ASEAN*. Paper presented for ADB/CEPI/KIEP Conference on Exchange Rate Regime in Emerging Market Economies, Tokyo, December 1999.

Dieter, Herbert (2000). *Monetary Regionalism: Regional Integration without Financial Crises*. Institute for Development and Peace, Duisberg University, May 2000.

Eichengreen, Barry (2005). 'Real and Pseudo Precondition for an Asian Monetary Union' in *Asian Economic Cooperation and Integration, Progress, Prospect, Challenges*. Asian Development Bank; Manila.

Mundell, Robert A. (1961). 'A Theory of Optimum Currency Areas.' *The American Economic Review*, 51; 4 (September 1961), pp.657–665.

Suseno. Sugiharso Safuan, Oentoro, Telisa Aulia Falianty, Yusuf Wibisono, Erna Sjafiiah W. (2006). *Joint Study on Single Currency in ASEAN-5*. Bank Indonesia and Bogor Agricultural University.

Watanabe, Shingho and Masanobu Ogura (2006). *How Far Apart Are Two ACUs from Each Other?: Asian Currency Unit and Asian Currency Union*. Bank of Japan Working Paper Series.

10 Regional financial arrangements in Asia

Jeffrey R. Shafer

Ten years after a brutal financial crisis, East Asia is once again leading the world in economic growth and development. Real incomes are above pre-crisis levels everywhere and in much of the region they are far higher. The policies adopted in each country created the conditions in which the energy and capacities of the people of the region could be remobilized. In the wake of the crisis we have seen the emergence of regional financial cooperation. I would take the view that this has played a secondary role to what has been done country by country in the region's strong turnaround, but this developing cooperation will be increasingly important going forward to keep the region on a strong, stable path and to counter quickly new financial strains should they arise. The threats to the East Asian economies will be different in the future than those that overwhelmed the region ten years ago. Then, the problem was that countries had become complacent about financial management after years of increasingly cheap financing in global markets. Short-term external debt built up, that debt was mostly in dollars, reserve levels were not raised to provide a cushion for financial reversals and fixed exchange rates became overvalued (following a strong U.S. dollar) with the result that many countries went into current account deficit. Banking systems were undercapitalized and had weak credit standards.

Those lessons have been learned. Debt is down. Short-term debt is down even more. Borrowing is increasingly in local currency; less in G-3 currencies. Reserves are more than ample, and when countries intervene it is to keep exchange rates down, not up, with the result that almost all current accounts are in surplus, some in very large surplus. Banking systems have been consolidated, recapitalized and professionalized. I would expect to see some easing back from the extraordinary financial conservatism that we see in East Asian countries today, but the painful lessons of 1997 will not be forgotten by the authorities in the region (I am less confident about the memory of the markets).

What are the threats to the Asian economies looking ahead? I see three:

1. An end to the present era of plentiful liquidity – market conditions that prompt frequent references to 1997 in the United States and in Europe. This will happen at some point although this is most likely two or three years down the road. The objective of Asian officials should be to build the capacity to absorb this shock when it comes without severe disruption of growth. I see them as well prepared.

2. A buildup of domestic imbalances within the countries of East Asia with asset inflation leading to bubbles in real estate and other fixed assets followed by collapse. The objective of Asian officials should be to deflate bubbles early. I am somewhat concerned about where countries in the region may be headed if excess global liquidity persists.

3. An unwinding of the large inter-regional current account imbalances (a $554 billion surplus for Asia – $167 billion Japan and $397 billion for the rest of Asia – with mainly the United States on the other side with a $850 billion deficit forecast by the IMF for 2007). At least a substantial narrowing of this imbalance is virtually certain, and a major exchange rate realignment will be part of the process. How soon and how orderly or disorderly is hard to say, but it is of critical importance for Asia that the adjustment be reasonably orderly so that it does not disrupt the emerging integrated Asian supply chain and become the trigger of an economic downturn in the region.

The development of financial cooperation within Asia will be critical for the successful management of these risks and other risks that are not so visible. There are other people who know much better than I do what has been done to develop financial cooperation in East Asia. My sense is that there has been important activity, but more could be done to build capacity to deal with the challenging times ahead. I am not one who believes that the rewards will come in the form of grand institutional achievements like a common Asian currency, but less dramatic accomplishments could make a big difference. Let me give an outsider's rough picture of what has been going on, subject to correction, and my sense of how the existing processes might be made more effective.

ASEAN+3, a Finance Ministry Group which has been particularly visible in leading the Chiang Mai initiative that established a network of reserve swaps, and the Asian Bond Market Initiative that has reduced impediments to the development of larger and deeper bond markets in the region and has instituted regional surveillance.

EMEAP – a central bankers group that led the creation of the Asian Bond Funds I and II. Sub-regional groups (SEACEN, for example) and supra-regional gathering (the APEC Finance Ministers comes to mind) and global institutions with regional focus (the BIS), have focused on regional financial issues.

The Asian Development Bank has provided support for financial cooperation. There have been some concrete developments. The swap network is one. I don't believe and I don't think its creators believe that, as an institutional development, this has fundamentally changed the prospects for financial management in the region. The amounts of money are too small and the strings attached are rightly too many to count for much in the face of the kind of pressure that can build up in modern markets. The Asian Bond Funds must similarly be seen as marginal developments in their impact on how markets work – too small and too constrained in structure by political considerations. (Investors in the region's currencies would want the new Taiwan dollar to be part of the portfolio, for example.)

The Asian Bond Market Initiative has made a bit more headway – benchmark yield curves have been established for example, but the ABMI has not yet broken down many of the barriers.

- Withholding taxes discourage cross-border investment
- hedging instruments are constrained by regulators
- multiple languages, clearing and settlement systems are barriers to market access
- slow, case-by-case, cross-border issuance approval is still the norm
- institutional investor bases are underdeveloped
- over 20 ratings agencies rate issues using different standards.

Still, it has taken more than four decades for the Euromarket to develop to its current maturity. We are in the early stages and the common focus of the financial officials in the region on this project is contributing to the step-by-step identification of obstacles to market growth and implementation of policies to remove them. There is a challenge not to fall behind developments in the global markets. I understand, for example, that there is a preoccupation among those working on the Asian Bond Market Initiative with the low liquidity of Asian markets when trading of bonds has virtually vanished in the United States. There, credit derivatives and interest rate swaps trade actively while the underlying securities stay put in portfolios of market makers.

While I do not see these concrete institutional achievements as transformational, I do think that the process by which they were achieved has been extremely important; and this importance is linked to the work in ASEAN+3 to establish a regional process of multilateral surveillance. I can't make a judgment on how strong this process is. It has been kept low-key and out of the limelight and I believe this is the right way to proceed. Frank exchanges on the policies of friends do not take place in public. Even if what is said in private does not alter policy directly, that conversations take place is important. The balance of academic work clearly supports the conclusion that I reached during 25 years in public service, either near or in the middle of surveillance and policy discussion: the gains from achieving the impossible dream of a fully globally optimal set of macroeconomic policies are small relative to what can be achieved in moving from where the world often is to a point of full information Nash equilibrium policies – each country does what is in its interest given what others are doing. This 'put your own house in order' approach can yield very good results. A good multilateral surveillance process provides two things that improve the Nash equilibrium:

- First, of course, it builds understanding of what others are planning and about how they think and are likely to respond given developments. This allows each country to make its decisions with better information about what others are doing and are likely to do.
- Second, the sharing of experience across countries and debate about its implications helps to build a better understanding among policymakers of how economies are likely to respond to different exogenous shocks and policy actions. The evolution and convergence of thinking among major old developed country policymakers has been strongly shaped over the years by discussions at the BIS and at the OECD, as well as in the G-7.

The entire agenda of regional multilateral cooperation – from the Chang Mai Initiative to the Asian Bond Market Initiative to the Asian Bond Funds, as well as surveillance, is serving to build a network in Asia at multiple levels, across countries and across agencies from finance ministries to central banks to financial regulators. People are getting to know each other. They are coming to understand how each other think and will react in different circumstances. This is a critical prerequisite to economic cooperation to deal with unexpected developments. I found when I was at the U.S. Treasury how much the relationships built up in the G-7, G-10 and WP-3 mattered when it was necessary to coordinate responses in a hurry. The bankruptcy of Barings was one occasion. The Mexican crisis was another.

The economic links between East Asian economies are becoming so close that this capacity is important for the region, just as it was in Europe long before there was a euro. The OEEC initially played this role, then the EEC provided a core European forum and the OECD a broader European one. The monthly BIS meetings provided opportunities for central banks to

122   *Jeffrey R. Shafer*

meet and talk. Now the EU has become virtually inclusive of Europe. East Asia needs to build similar networks and that is happening. East Asia needs to be plugged into the global multilateral process too. Progress is being made: China is routinely invited now to take part in G-7 meetings as a guest, reinforcing Japan's charter membership. Singapore and Hong Kong are members of the Financial Stability forum, a very important global body focused on the safety and soundness of global financial markets, but more needs to be done to bring Asia into the global system.

China should be a full member of the G-7, or, as I and others have proposed, in a G-4 comprised of the U.S., the euro-area, Japan and China. As a guest, China is not systematically included in the deputies and working-level meetings where many of the most important discussions take place. Full Chinese participation in the G-7 or a successor would plug East Asia more closely into global surveillance and strengthen the developing regional surveillance process. Using APEC as a forum for surveillance would also give all countries in the region access to U.S. officials as well as some others outside Asia as the OECD did for Europe, but APEC is becoming a bit large and does not engage central banks.

I am very positive about what I see happening to develop regional cooperation; but in one respect Asia seems to be repeating the history of the G-7 and G-10 and this concerns me. The G-7 started as a G-5 of finance ministers. Central bank governors were quickly invited to join but only at the level of Ministers and Governors. The deputies who prepared initiatives like the Plaza Agreement and the Louvre Accord in the 1980s did not bring in central banks. Since monetary policies are the policy instruments that most strongly affect exchange rates (much more powerfully than sterilized foreign exchange market intervention in the absence of pervasive capital controls), these agreements depended critically on central banks' support.

The strains were evident in OECD meetings of the WP-3 where the G-7 deputies meet with the central bank counterparts in only a slightly larger set of countries. There were sharp exchanges in the second half of the 1980s, not so often between countries, but between central bankers, who had come to see their objective as being to establish and maintain price stability, taken to mean low, stable inflation, and the finance ministers who had made commitments to manage exchange rates. These objectives did not always coincide. It was not a great period for international cooperation with obvious tensions triggering the global stock market collapse of October 19, 1987 and Japan going down the path of the bubble economy. It is fine for central banks and finance ministries to meet in their own circles to discuss their parochial interests, but macroeconomic surveillance needs to be a collective undertaking fully involving both. The picture that I get is that the finance ministries and central banks in East Asia are forming distant clubs.

I think it will be important to form a common grouping that meets regularly at the level of Ministers and Governors, prepared by meetings at deputies and deputies' deputies levels.

With this, I believe that East Asia will have the framework within which to develop clearer economic cooperation along several lines. I see this as especially important for managing the coming exchange rate and current account adjustment with the rest of the world. It will be critical that as this happens there not only be close consultation in the G-7 + or a G-4, but that there be close regional cooperation to maintain order in regional exchange rate relationships as Asia's exchange rates adjust vis-à-vis the dollar and euro. It is a problem that Europe faced in the 1970s and it led to the creation of the EMS. I am not sure that this structure is the model to follow, but I am sure that only with close active consultation among the central banks and finance ministries of the region will the best path be found.

11 Six notable features of macroeconomic performance in post-crisis Asia*,[1]

Shinji Takagi

In this presentation, I will highlight the following six notable features of Asia's macroeconomic performance over the past ten years:

- Growth quickly recovered in most of emerging Asia, but potential growth has likely declined.
- China and, to a lesser extent, India emerged as the region's economic powers.
- Current account balances turned from deficit to surplus in much of emerging Asia.
- Emerging Asia accumulated a significant amount of international reserves.
- Investment declined in most emerging Asia, but not in China or India.
- Exchange rate flexibility increased in some countries, but in most the currencies remained stable against the US dollar.

In highlighting these features, my focus is on China and six other major economies: Indonesia, Korea, Malaysia, the Philippines, Taiwan, and Thailand. As appropriate, I will also make references to other Asian economies, including Japan, India, Hong Kong, Singapore, Myanmar, Vietnam, and Lao PDR.

Growth quickly recovered in most of emerging Asia, but potential growth has likely declined

Economic recovery from the crisis was relatively quick for most adversely affected countries, but growth did not return to the pre-crisis level. For six major countries (see Figure 11.1) (Indonesia, Korea, Malaysia, the Philippines, Taiwan, and Thailand), for example, economic growth declined from 7–8 percent during 1994–1996 to 4–6 percent during 2003–2005. Lower potential growth is not as clear for Hong Kong, which recently came

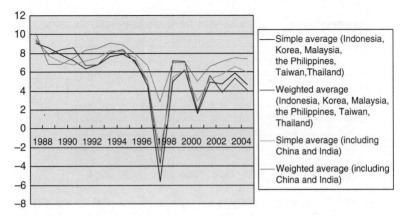

Figure 11.1 Real GDP growth in selected Asian countries (in percent per year).

out of recession; or the Philippines, whose economic growth since the crisis has been subject to large swings.

On the other hand, lower income countries continued to maintain their growth momentum: Cambodia continued to grow at a rapid pace (over 10 percent per year during 2004–2006); the rate of growth in Lao PDR during 2004–2006 (at or over 7 percent) was about one percentage point higher than the growth experienced during 2001–2003; Myanmar's growth remained at 11–14 percent during 2001–2006; and Vietnam's GDP grew at 7–8 percent during 2001–2006.

China and, to a lesser extent, India emerged as the region's economic powers

The growth performance of China and India stands out. China maintained its growth momentum (though slower than the initial take-off phase of 1992–1994 and somewhat moderating in the latter years), while growth picked up in India – China's growth during 2003–2006 was slightly over 10 percent per year and India's growth averaged more than 8 percent per year during the same period. There was thus a polarization of growth performance between these 'newer' emerging market economies and the 'older' ones (as indicated below, this also shows up in investment performance, with implications for future potential growth).[2] As a result, as indicated in Figures 11.2 and 11.3, the share of China in Asia's total GDP (excluding Japan) rose from around 25 percent at the beginning of the 1990s to almost

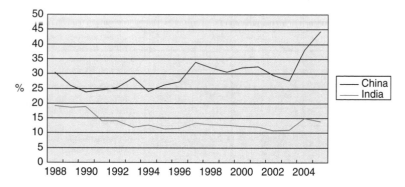

Figure 11.2 The emergence of China and India (as percent of Asia's total GDP).

45 percent in 2005. The share of India fluctuated between 10 and 15 percent of the region's GDP, but the less prominent rise of India is in part an artifact of the faster growth of China. When we exclude China from the region's total GDP, India's share rises to 25 percent. Together, China and India account for 60 percent of Asia's total output.

Current account balances turned from deficit to surplus in much of emerging Asia

Immediately after the crisis, the affected countries needed to generate large current account surpluses as a counterpart of large capital outflows. Even after recovery from the crisis had set in, these and other economies

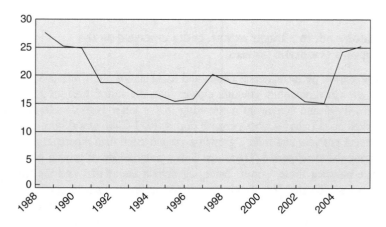

Figure 11.3 The share of India in Asia's GDP (percent: excl. China).

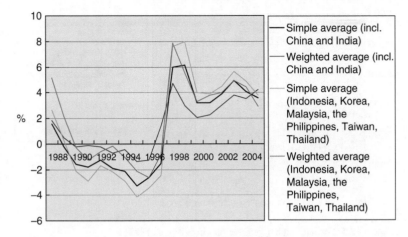

Figure 11.4 Current account balances in selected Asian countries (in percent of GDP).

continued to run (sometimes large) current account surpluses. For six major countries (see Figure 11.4) (Indonesia, Korea, Malaysia, the Philippines, Taiwan, and Thailand), for example, the current account balance turned from a deficit of 2–4 percent of GDP during 1994–1996 to a surplus of 4–6 percent during 2003–2005.

China, Hong Kong, Malaysia, and Singapore experienced a particularly sharp widening of the current account surpluses. In 2005, China had a surplus of over 7 percent of GDP (up from 3.5 percent in 2004), Singapore 28 percent of GDP, Malaysia 15 percent of GDP, and Hong Kong 11 percent of GDP. On the other hand, India, Indonesia, Korea, Taiwan, and Thailand saw a decline in the most recent years; Thailand's current account is now in deficit. The current account of Indonesia is in approximate balance.

Emerging Asia accumulated a significant amount of international reserves

With current account surpluses, and resumption of capital inflows in some cases, most countries of Asia accumulated foreign exchange reserves. The foreign exchange reserves of nine major countries (see Figure 11.5) (Hong Kong, India, Indonesia, Korea, Malaysia, the Philippines, Singapore, Taiwan, and Thailand), for example, rose from $170 billion at the end

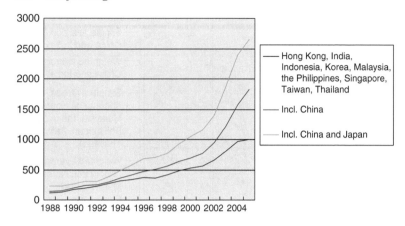

Figure 11.5 Foreign exchange reserves (in billions of US$).

of 1990 (and $370 billion at the end of 1996) to over $1 trillion at the end of 2005. With China, the total amount increased from $200 billion at the end of 1990 to $1.8 trillion at the end of 2005. In addition to Japan and China, Taiwan ($250 billion), Korea ($210 billion), India ($130 billion), Hong Kong ($125 billion), and Singapore ($115 billion) had over $100 billion in foreign exchange reserves.

The countries that accumulated significant foreign exchange reserves include: China, Hong Kong, India, Korea, Malaysia, Singapore, Taiwan, and Thailand. Most significantly, China added over $200 billion each in 2004 and 2005, with the balance now exceeding $1 trillion. In contrast, the reserve accumulations in Indonesia and the Philippines were more modest. Though the amount was small, Cambodia, Laos, Myanmar, and Vietnam were also net accumulators.

Investment declined in most emerging Asia, but not in China or India

Along with economic recovery, investment also recovered from the sharp decline experienced at the time of the crisis, but never back to pre-crisis levels (see Figure 11.6). Higher income countries (Hong Kong, Korea, Malaysia, and Singapore), in particular, reduced investment considerably (by roughly ten percentage points on average). Thailand saw a recent pickup in investment, but the level is still low (20–30 percent of GDP),

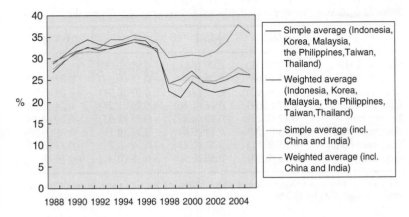

Figure 11.6 Gross capital formation in selected Asian countries (in percent of GDP).

compared to the pre-crisis period (around or over 40 percent of GDP). In Malaysia, private investment declined noticeably as a percent of GDP.

This is not the case with lower income countries (Cambodia, China, India, and Vietnam) – they increased investment or maintained a high level of investment, as they should. Although gross capital formation in China declined somewhat in the latter years, it is still the highest among the major countries (44 percent of GDP in 2005). More worrisome are the Philippines and Indonesia. Gross capital formation in the Philippines declined from over 20 percent of GDP in 2000 to less than 16 percent in 2005, while gross capital formation in Indonesia in 2005 was 22 percent of GDP, compared to the range of 30–32 percent in the 1990s prior to the crisis.

Exchange rate flexibility increased in some countries, but in most the currencies remained stable against the US dollar

Following the crisis, and especially in more recent years, greater exchange rate flexibility was introduced. Compared to the exchange rate behavior prior to the crisis, as well as to the behavior of the dollar-yen rate as a benchmark, the flexibility of the Indonesian rupiah, the Korean won, and the Thai baht appeared clearly to have increased. Most other currencies (see Table 11.1), however, remained relatively stable against the US dollar, including the currencies of lower income countries (Vietnam, Lao PDR, and Cambodia).

Table 11.1 Monthly movements of selected Asian currencies against the US dollar

	1995/96	2001/02	2003/04	2005/06
Chinese RMB	−0.03 (0.01)	0.00 (0.00)	−0.00 (0.00)	−0.11 (0.04)
Indian rupee	0.25 (0.68)	0.05 (0.04)	−0.18 (0.37)	0.03 (0.47)
Indonesian rupiah	0.14 (0.02)	−0.13 (7.08)	0.07 (0.91)	−0.05 (0.98)
Japanese yen	0.27 (2.69)	0.08 (1.66)	−0.26 (1.25)	0.24 (0.52)
Korean won	0.12 (0.21)	−0.12 (0.97)	−0.25 (1.03)	−0.19 (0.44)
Philippine peso	0.13 (0.20)	0.11 (0.64)	0.11 (0.18)	−0.25 (0.39)
Singapore dollar	−0.08 (0.11)	0.52 (0.45)	−0.11 (0.23)	−0.12 (0.22)
Thai baht	0.04 (0.04)	−0.50 (0.50)	−0.18 (0.34)	−0.15 (0.57)

Logarithmic differences; Figures are averages multiplied by 100; those in parentheses are variances multiplied by 10,000.

Issues for discussion

- Do the large persistent current account surpluses – coupled with sluggish investment at home – present a type of market failure? If so, why and how?
- What can be done to invest the region's 'surplus funds' more productively within the region? Is there a regional solution?
- Is the lower investment in many Asian countries (compared with the pre-crisis years) an optimal response to lower expected future growth?
- Would the large accumulation of foreign exchange reserves translate into higher inflation (at least in some countries)? What would be the implications for these countries of allowing the nominal exchange rate to appreciate?

Notes

* Prepared for presentation at the conference 'A Decade Later: Asia's New Responsibilities in the International Monetary System', Seoul, May 2–3, 2007.
1 All underlying data come from ADB and IMF.
2 This asymmetric growth performance may well reflect, to some extent, the competitive relationship of these two groups of countries in the export markets.

Index

Page references followed by f indicate an illustrative figure; t indicates a table

China and Asia
Economic and Financial Interactions
Yin-Wong Cheung, University of California, USA
and **Kar-Yiu Wong,** University of Washington, USA

It is difficult to overstate the growing importance of China and Asia in the global economy. Despite the sharp downturn experienced in the 1997 financial crisis, China and Asia have bounced back strongly in the new millennium and experienced solid economic growth. In this book, Ying-Wong Cheung and Kar-Yiu Wong have gathered together 35 renowned researchers from four continents to examine contemporary issues in economic and financial interactions, with a focus on China and Asia.

Contents: Introduction 1. WTO and Development: It's All About Mercantilist Game 2. Liberalization of Agricultural Trade: Path to Development or Chasing a Mirage? 3. Deepening of the GATS: Need for Cautious Treading 4. WTO and Trade Facilitation: Some Implications 5. Competition Policy at the WTO: Right Diagnosis but Wrong Prescription 6. Multilateral Framework on Investment: Much Pain Without Gain! 7. As if TRIPS Was Not Enough 8. WTO and Environment: Think Locally, Act Globally? 9. Resisting the Expansion: Experiences and Possible Implications 10. Evolving a Trade Regime for Development: Some Considerations

December 2008: 234x156: 288pp
Hb: 978-0-415-77609-7: **£80.00 $160.00**

Routledge Studies in Modern World Economy Series

Routledge books are available from all good bookshops, or may be ordered by calling Taylor and Francis Direct Sales on +44(0)1235 400524 (credit card orders) For more information please contact Gemma Anderson on +44 (0) 207 017 6192 or email gemma.anderson@tandf.co.uk

Expanding Frontiers of Global Trade Rules
The Political Economy Dynamics of the International Trading System

Nitya Nitya

This book analyses one of the most controversial areas in the political economy of international trade, namely the issues surrounding the creation of new 'trade rules'. Various concerns are addressed, including the environment, labour standards, intellectual property rights, trade facilitation, competition policy, investment and government procurement, to many conventional trade topics including the trade and development linkage.

Contents: Introduction 1. WTO and Development: It's All About Mercantilist Game 2. Liberalization of Agricultural Trade: Path to Development or Chasing a Mirage? 3. Deepening of the GATS: Need for Cautious Treading 4. WTO and Trade Facilitation: Some Implications 5. Competition Policy at the WTO: Right Diagnosis but Wrong Prescription 6. Multilateral Framework on Investment: Much Pain Without Gain! 7. As if TRIPS Was Not Enough 8. WTO and Environment: Think Locally, Act Globally? 9. Resisting the Expansion: Experiences and Possible Implications 10. Evolving a Trade Regime for Development: Some Considerations

February 2008: 234x156: 224pp
Hb: 978-0-415-44295-4: **£70.00 $140.00**

Routledge Studies in Modern World Economy

Routledge books are available from all good bookshops, or may be ordered by calling Taylor and Francis Direct Sales on +44(0)1235 400524 (credit card orders) For more information please contact Gemma Anderson on +44 (0) 207 017 6192 or email gemma.anderson@tandf.co.uk

Review of Political Economy

Increase in pages for 2008

EDITORS:
Gary Mongiovi, *St John's University, USA*
Steve Pressman, *Monmouth University, USA*

The **Review of Political Economy** is a peer-reviewed journal
welcoming constructive and critical contributions in all areas of
political economy, including the Austrian, Behavioral Economics,
Feminist Economics, Institutionalist, Marxian, Post Keynesian,
and Sraffian traditions. The **Review** publishes both theoretical and
empirical research, and is also open to submissions in methodology,
economic history and the history of economic thought that cast light
on issues of contemporary relevance in political economy. Comments
on articles published in the **Review** are encouraged.

SUBSCRIPTION RATES
Volume 20, 2008, 4 issues per year
Print ISSN 0953-8259
Online ISSN 1465-3982
Institutional rate (print and online): US$836; £487; €669
Institutional rate (online access only): US$794; £462; €635
Personal rate (print only): US$194; £120; €155

   A world of specialist information for the academic, professional and business
communities. To find out more go to: **www.informaworld.com**

    Register your email address at **www.informaworld.com/eupdates** to receive information
on books, journals and other news within your areas of interest.

For further information, please contact Customer Services at either of the following:
T&F Informa UK Ltd, Sheepen Place, Colchester, Essex, CO3 3LP, UK
Tel: +44 (0) 20 7017 5544 Fax: 44 (0) 20 7017 5198
Email: tf.enquiries@informa.com Website: www.tandf.co.uk/journals
Taylor & Francis Inc, 325 Chestnut Street, 8th Floor, Philadelphia, PA 19106, USA
Tel: +1 800 354 1420 (toll-free calls from within the US)
or +1 215 625 8900 (calls from overseas) Fax: +1 215 625 2940
Email: customerservice@taylorandfrancis.com Website: www.taylorandfrancis.com

When ordering, please quote: XJ04601A

View an online sample issue at:
www.informaworld.com/ROPE

The Journal of International Trade & Economic Development

An International and Comparative Review

Now included in the Thomson ISI Social Sciences Citation Index ©

EDITORS:
Professor Pasquale M. Sgro, *Deakin Business School, Australia*
Professor Bharat R. Hazari, *City University of Hong Kong, Hong Kong*

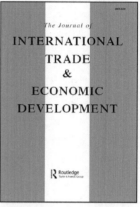

The Journal of International Trade & Economic Development, a peer-reviewed journal, focuses on international economics, economic development and, more importantly, the interface between trade and development. The links between trade and development economics are critical at a time when both fluctuating commodity prices and trade liberalisation and agreements can radically affect the economies of developing countries.

The Journal of International Trade & Economic Development is designed to meet the needs of international and development economists, economic historians, applied economists and policy makers. The international experts who make up the journal's Editorial Board encourage contributions from economists world-wide.

SUBSCRIPTION RATES
Volume 17, 2008, 4 issues per year
Print ISSN 0963-8199
Online ISSN 1469-9559
Institutional rate (print and online): US$931; £564; €745
Institutional rate (online access only): US$884; £535; €707
Personal rate (print only): US$142; £97; €114

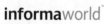

A world of specialist information for the academic, professional and business communities. To find out more go to: **www.informaworld.com**

Register your email address at **www.informaworld.com/eupdates** to receive information on books, journals and other news within your areas of interest.

For further information, please contact Customer Services at either of the following:
T&F Informa UK Ltd, Sheepen Place, Colchester, Essex, CO3 3LP, UK
Tel: +44 (0) 20 7017 5544 Fax: 44 (0) 20 7017 5198
Email: tf.enquiries@informa.com Website: www.tandf.co.uk/journals
Taylor & Francis Inc, 325 Chestnut Street, 8th Floor, Philadelphia, PA 19106, USA
Tel: +1 800 354 1420 (toll-free calls from within the US)
or +1 215 625 8900 (calls from overseas) Fax: +1 215 625 2940
Email: customerservice@taylorandfrancis.com Website: www.taylorandfrancis.com

When ordering, please quote: XJ04201A

View an online sample issue at:
www.informaworld.com/JITED